1 - His Face Shone Like the Sun

HIS FACE
SHONE LIKE THE SUN

**Encountering The
Transfigured Christ In Scripture**

HIS FACE
SHONE LIKE THE SUN

Encountering The
Transfigured Christ In Scripture

by

ROBERT WILD

* * *

"This is my beloved Son,
with whom I am well pleased; listen to him."
Mt 17:5

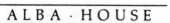
ALBA · HOUSE   alba house   NEW · YORK

SOCIETY OF ST. PAUL, 2187 VICTORY BLVD., STATEN ISLAND, NEW YORK 10314

Library of Congress Cataloging in Publication Data

Wild, Robert A.,   1936—
  His Face shone like the sun.

  1. Jesus Christ — Transfiguration.   2. Jesus Christ —
Person and offices.   3. Spiritual life.   I. Title.

BT410.W55   1986   232.9'56   86-8054
ISBN 0-8189-0501-8

Designed, printed and bound in the United States of
America by the Fathers and Brothers of the
Society of St. Paul, 2187 Victory Boulevard,
Staten Island, New York 10314, as part of their
communications apostolate.

1 2 3 4 5 6 7 8 9 (Current Printing: first digit)

*Dedicated to everyone
who opens the Sacred Scriptures, that
the Word may dwell in them.*

PREFACE

IN CHAPTER 24 of St. Luke's Gospel, we have laid down for us the principles upon which all Christian reading of the Scriptures is based. We read there that Cleopas and another disciple of Jesus had left Jerusalem and were walking toward Emmaus when Jesus drew near to them and asked them what they were discussing.

> ". . .Jesus of Nazareth, a prophet powerful in word and deed in the eyes of God and all the people; how our chief priests and leaders delivered him up to be condemned to death and crucified him. We were hoping that he was the one who would set Israel free. . . Some of our number went to the tomb and found it to be just as the women said, but him they did not see."

> And then he said to them, "What little sense you have! How slow you are to believe all that the prophets have announced! Did not the Messiah have to undergo all this so as to enter his glory?" Beginning then with Moses and all the prophets, he interpreted for them every passage of Scripture which referred to him. (Lk 24:19-27)

The rest of the story is familiar. The disciples prevailed upon the stranger to stay with them, and then, in the breaking of the bread, they knew it was Jesus. As they hurried back to tell the other disciples, they said to one another:

"Were not our hearts burning inside us as he talked to us on the road and explained the Scriptures to us?" (Lk 24:32)

When they arrived back at Jerusalem and began to speak to the other disciples, Jesus appeared in their midst and spoke to them, proving that it was really he risen from the dead.

> Then he said to them: "Recall those words I spoke to you when I was still with you: everything written about me in the law of Moses and the prophets and psalms had to be fulfilled." Then he opened their minds to the understanding of the Scriptures. (Lk 24:44-45)

We see in these passages some very fundamental laws regarding the understanding of the Sacred Text. First, notice that Jesus appears where the brethren are assembled. This he promised to do: "Where two or three are gathered in my name, there I am in their midst" (Mt 18:20). In the instances just recorded, we see first the two disciples together, not realizing that Jesus was the third one in their group. Then, back in Jerusalem, the brethren are gathered together. Their faith is still imperfect, but Jesus appears in their midst and proves to them his risen reality.

Secondly, the understanding of the Scriptures is linked to a living grasp of the mystery of the death and resurrection of Jesus Christ. The Scriptures are the account of the working out of God's plan of salvation. They tell us how this plan of salvation touched and reached God's people through all the centuries of preparation until it burst forth in all the splendor and the light of its glory in the death and resurrection of Jesus, the Son of God. It is absolutely impossible to understand the Scriptures if one's mind has not been touched by this mystery. Since the Scriptures are meant to reveal to us God as he works out his plan of salvation, they remain a closed book to us unless our lives are in an ever-deepening way entering into that mystery, that plan of salvation, which God had in mind from all eternity. That is why we see in Chapter 24 of St. Luke's Gospel the fact that it is the risen Jesus who opens the minds of the disciples to the understanding of the Scriptures.

The third principle that we gather from this event is that real understanding of the Scriptures does not come from human resources alone but is fundamentally the result of the divine initiative. It was *Jesus* who explained to the two disciples on the way to Emmaus that the Messiah had to suffer and thus enter into his glory. It was *Jesus* who opened the minds of the disciples to the understanding of the Scriptures. Therefore, we must understand that the heart of understanding the Scriptures is prayer, prayer to the Lord Jesus Christ in all his reality and majesty, begging him through the work of the Holy Spirit to take the initiative and open our minds, detaching them from our preoccupation with self and the world so that we can enter into the glories of his mystery.

The fourth and last principle that is alluded to in the Lukan text is this, that the full recognition of Jesus comes in the breaking of the bread. We read in Luke 24:31 that, after Jesus had taken bread, blessed it, broken it, and distributed it, "with that their eyes were opened, and they recognized him. . ." It is in the celebration of the Eucharist that the Scriptures find their fulfillment. It is at that moment when the brethren are gathered together to praise God that the word of God is proclaimed and Jesus himself manifests his Gospel. This is clearly stated in the Second Vatican Council. Speaking of the ways that Christ is present to us when we gather for the liturgy, the Document on the Liturgy says: "Christ is present in his word since it is himself who speaks when the Holy Scriptures are read in the Church"

(Document on the Liturgy, #7). In another document, the Vatican Council goes so far as to say concerning the context of the Eucharist: "Hence the Eucharist shows itself to be the source and the apex of the whole work of preaching the Gospel" (Document on Priests, #5).

Let no one think, however, that the Vatican Council or any Church teaching wishes to discourage people from the earnest application of their minds to a deep understanding of the Scriptures, learning as much about them as they can. It is interesting that St. Therese of Lisieux, who herself was not a scholarly person, had such respect for this aspect of understanding the Scriptures that she once said: "If I had been a priest, I should have made a thorough study of Hebrew and Greek so as to understand the thought of God as he has vouchsafed to express it in our human language."

This is easy to understand. When we love someone, we want to know as much about them as possible, and we want to apply our minds as energetically as possible to understanding what they have said. The Scriptures are a letter from God to mankind, and, just as we would read a letter from someone we love with great care and read it over and over again, trying to understand all the shades of meaning that this beloved person had put in his words to us, so it is with the efforts to understand the word of God.

The very existence of the Council itself bears eloquent witness to the fruit of the biblical studies and other studies which preceded it. The result of the Council has been an ever-increasing number of good translations into the vernacular languages so that all of God's people can apply themselves to an understanding of the text. All of this, of course, is due to the scholarly work of those who have been called by God to this task.

Nevertheless, it remains true that the heart of understanding the Scriptures lies not so much in a grasp of what is being *said* as in an understanding of *what the text is talking about.* The text is talking about God, about his plan of salvation, about the wonder and beauty of our Lord Jesus Christ, and about the mysterious work of the Holy Spirit who has been given to us who believe as "the first fruit of our salvation."

It is, thus, a pleasure for me to introduce this book by my brother in the Lord, Father Robert Wild. In it he sets forth some of the witnesses of tradition and modern times concerning the need for reading the Scriptures and the fruit that can be derived from an earnest faith application of our minds to the Sacred Text. I make my own this prayer which Paul once uttered as I ask God to bless all those who will read this book:

Everything written before our times was written for our instruction, that we might derive hope from the lessons of patience and the words of encouragement in the Scriptures. May God, the source of all patience and encouragement, enable you to live in perfect harmony with one another according to the spirit of Christ Jesus so that with one heart and voice you may glorify God, the Father of our Lord Jesus Christ. (Rm 15:4-6)

FATHER FRANCIS MARTIN
Mother of God Community
Feast of St. Mark the Evangelist
April 25, 1986

CONTENTS

Preface vii

Introduction xvii

I "After Six Days. . ."
   Scripture As An Epiphany Of Christ 3

II "Jesus Took With Him. . ."
    Scripture As Daily, Intimate Conversation with
    Christ 11

III "Peter, James and John. . ."
     Hearing The Word As Members Of The Church 19

IV "Led Them Up A High Mountain Apart
    By Themselves"
    Encountering Christ Alone 27

V ". . . To Pray. And As He Was Praying"
   Praying The Scriptures 35

VI "He Was Transfigured Before Them,
    And His Face Shone Like The Sun,
    And His Garments Became White As Light"
    Meeting The Glorious Christ In The Scriptures 43

VII   "And Behold Two Men Talked With Him,
       Moses And Elijah"
       The Whole Of Scripture Is Only One Word:
       Christ 51

VIII   "They were Talking About His Exodus"
       Scripture As Exodus Into Christ 59

IX   "And A Voice Came Out Of The Cloud,
       'This Is My Beloved Son With Whom I Am
       Well-Pleased. Listen To Him'"
       Listening To Christ In The Scriptures
       Is Obeying Him 67

X   "Peter And His Companions Were
       Very Sleepy, But When They Woke Up
       They Saw His Glorious Appearance"
       Sin As Obscuring The Light Of The
       Glorious Christ 77

XI   "A Bright Cloud Overshadowed Them, And
       They Were Afraid As They Entered The Cloud"
       Awe and Reverence In Approaching The Scriptures . . 85

XII   "Master, It Is Good For Us To Be Here.
       Let Us Put Up Three Tents. . ."
       Scripture As A Call To Painful Mission 93

XIII   "When the Disciples Heard This
       They Fell On Their Faces"
       Approaching Christ In The Scriptures As Sinners . . 101

XIV   "But Jesus Came And Touched Them. 'Get Up,'
       He Said. 'Don't Be Afraid'"

The Touch Of Jesus Is Necessary To Hear The Scriptures 109

Appendix A   The Three Synoptic Accounts
              Of The Transfiguration 117

Appendix B   Key To Quoted Works Of Origen 119

Appendix C   Excerpts From *Dei Verbum*, The
              Dogmatic Constitution On
              Divine Revelation 121

INTRODUCTION

In John 5 Jesus makes a distinction between *studying* the Scriptures and having the Word of God *dwell within* the person: "You diligently study the Scriptures because you think that by them you possess eternal life" (5:39). "You have never heard his voice nor seen his form, nor does his word dwell in you, for you do not believe the one he sent" (5:37-39). It is possible to study the Scriptures without seeing and hearing the Lord with our spiritual senses: without, consequently, having the Word *dwell in us*, transforming our hearts and our lives. This book is entirely concerned with the attitudes of mind and heart necessary for allowing the Word to dwell in us. The formal study of the Scriptures, with original languages, commentaries, etc., has a place, but without our active listening and responding, the Word will not dwell in us.

Scripture itself offers several images for this indwelling of the Word. One such image is that of eating food: "Man does not live on bread alone," says Jesus to Satan, quoting Dt 8:3, "but on every word that comes from the mouth of God" (Mt 4:4). Using the same image, the Word of God is a scroll which the prophets are bidden to eat:

> And he said to me, "Son of man, eat what is before you, eat this Scroll; then go and speak to the house of Israel." So I opened my mouth, and he gave me the scroll to eat. . . So I ate it, and it tasted as sweet as honey in my mouth. Ezk 3:1-3

Still using this image, the primary way of taking the Word of God into our spiritual mouths is through *faith*. The Word of God is then digested through all the attitudes portrayed in the Bible in its description of people's en-counters with God. Some of these attitudes I propose to treat here. Finally, food is ultimately assimilated into our systems by life, by activity. Thus the *doing* of the Word of God is the final act of appropriation: "Why do you call me 'Lord, Lord,' and not *do* what I say?" (Lk 6:46).

Using still another image, Scripture speaks of "un-circumcised ears":

> To whom can I speak and give warning? Who will listen to me? Their ears are uncircumcised so they cannot hear. The word of the Lord is offensive to them; they find no pleasure in it.   Jr 6:10

> You stiff-necked people with uncircumcised hearts and ears! You are just like your fathers; you always resist the Holy Spirit!   Ac 7:51

If we think of the Word of God as a sword (Heb 4:12), as a knife, then it is this knife which can circumcise our spiritual ears and hearts to allow the Word to transform us. Faith, then, is total openness to this "operation" of the Spirit, allowing the sword of the Spirit to penetrate and cut into the hardness of our hearts.

One of the most oft-quoted prophetic passages in the New Testament — quoted by Christ himself — refers to the *mere* hearing, the *mere* looking, at the Word of God without personal appropriation:

> You will be ever hearing but never understanding;
> You will be ever seeing but never perceiving.

For this peoples' heart has become calloused;
they hardly hear with their ears,
and they have closed their eyes.

Otherwise they might see with their eyes,
hear with their ears,
understand with their hearts,
and turn, and I would heal them.   Is 6:9-11

In this book I do not in any way intend to be negative towards Scripture studies. They have a place; I have profited very much from them myself. But such study must be done with *faith.*

There is a sense in which the Scriptures cannot be studied, if by "study" we mean an attempt to encompass it with our minds. We can never fully understand the Word of God in this way since we are ultimately called to "stand under" the Word, allowing the Word to judge our lives instead of us judging the Word. To "understand" is to "stand under" the light of God and allow this light to judge and illumine our lives. Kierkegaard said that the only possible way to relate to the Word of God is to obey it.

Studies without faith seek to put ourselves in control of the text, while faith (which can be combined with study) seeks to put ourselves in submission to the Word's meaning. The goal is a spiritual understanding — the eating, the assimilation of the Word into our circumcised hearts so that God can reveal himself and gradually penetrate and transform our whole lives. All study must lead to this growth of spiritual understanding. Studies *can* be a purely human enterprise; spiritual understanding can only come from God.

The Bible is not just another book to be studied as a

"form of literature" along with other holy books of the world. Even if it is so studied, its uniqueness and truly divine character must not be lost sight of. Thus, the proper spiritual attitudes of approaching God in the Scriptures are absolutely essential, while Scripture studies are secondary and meant to *foster* these attitudes. Otherwise we will be "hearing without understanding, seeing but never perceiving," and we will come under the censure of Christ who said that we are studying the Scriptures but they are not in us:

> "If I had not come and spoken to them, they would not have any sin; but now they have no excuse for their sin" (Jn 15:22). The only thing that this can really mean is that the Logos is saying that, on the one hand, those within whom he has not yet come to fullness have no sin, but those who after already having had part in him act contrary to the ideas by which he comes to fullness in us, are guilty of sin.   Origen, *Commentary on John* SF, 150 *

A greater judgment will be ours who have often heard the words of the Gospel but have not put them into practice.

I have just quoted Origen. I will be quoting him throughout this book. A secondary purpose of this little book is to help us regain the "mind of the Fathers" towards the Scriptures. The Fathers were men of faith, and their great faith guided their scriptural interpretations — although at the same time, many of them such as Origen and Jerome were profound Scripture scholars.

When Origen says that the white garments of Christ on Tabor were the words of the Gospel, we see this as "piety," but not the "real meaning of the text." I personally don't believe it's possible to discover *the meaning* to a text. I think

---

* See Appendix B for Key to Origen's writings.

this is an intellectual trap. Ten people could prayerfully read, "I am the bread of life" and, because of their personal relationship with God, arrive (through the grace of the Holy Spirit) at ten different meanings. Each meaning could be true, valid, and inspired by God. To say there is only one, definite meaning is a prejudice of our scientific mind.

Each text is only the beginning of a living dialogue between the Holy Spirit and each person. If a person is open in living faith to that text, the Holy Spirit will teach him or her *the truth* about that text for his or her spiritual life. This personal truth is not *less than* the presumed scientific conclusion. When we approach the Scriptures in faith we are not primarily engaged in studying a text or seeking for a "fixed meaning." We are meeting a Person who can communicate to us personally any number of meanings for our daily spiritual needs. It is *this* which is and *must* be available to all. This approach does not negate the importance of Scripture studies, which in any case are of benefit for all and not only for professional scholars. God wishes to speak with *everyone* himself.

The Fathers were geniuses in their openness to the Holy Spirit, allowing him to teach them the deep, spiritual meaning of the Word of God. For them, the Scriptures were another incarnation of the Word, similar to the Eucharist. Just as Christ's real Body and Blood is eaten in the Eucharist, so too, when Scripture is received in faith and love, we are really and truly eating the Word. Listen again to the great Origen:

> Just as this spoken word cannot, according to its own na-
> ture, be touched or seen, but when written in a book and, so
> to speak, become bodily, then indeed is seen and touched,
> so too is it with the fleshless and bodiless Word of God:
> according to its divinity it is neither seen nor written;

but when it becomes flesh, it is seen and written. Therefore
. . . it has become flesh.   *Commentary on Matthew*

You are, therefore, to understand the Scriptures in this
way: as the one, perfect body of the Word.   *Commentary on
John* SF, 153, 156

The Fathers feasted on this Word of God in the
Scriptures as very few others in the history of Christianity.
We must learn again to approach the Scriptures as they did
— in faith and in the Holy Spirit.

The substance of what follows was originally presented
at the new Catholic Bible College in Canmore, Alberta. With
a Bible on her lap, Clair, the young (age 10) daughter of
Louis and Susanne Stoeckle, the directors, sat through an
hour's summary of my talks. Privately, later on, her father
asked her what she got out of the talk.

She thought for a moment and said: "Well, he said that if
you love Jesus and do what he said then whooosh! you will
become the same color as Jesus!" This is an *exact* summary of
all I had been trying to say that week. See how the Spirit
enlightens the little ones!

Origen

Commentary on the Song of Songs
ACW, 61-62

"Since the soul does not find (in instructions from her masters and teachers) the full and perfect satisfaction of her desire and love, let her pray that her pure and virginal mind may be enlightened by the illumination and the visitation of the Word of God himself. For, when her mind is filled with divine perception and understanding, without the agency of human or angelic ministration, then she may believe she has received the kisses of the Word of God himself.

"For this reason, then, and for the sake of these kisses, let the soul say in her prayers to God: 'Let him kiss me with the kisses of his mouth.' For as long as she was incapable of receiving the solid and unadulterated doctrine of the Word of God himself, of necessity she received 'kisses,' that is, interpretations, from the mouths of teachers. But, when she has begun to discern for herself what was obscure, to unravel what was tangled, to unfold what was involved, to interpret parables and riddles and the sayings of the wise along the lines of her own expert thinking, then let her believe that she has now received the kisses of the Spouse himself, that is, the Word of God.

"Moreover, the plural 'kisses' is used in order that we may understand that the lighting up of every obscure meaning is a kiss of the Word of God bestowed on the perfected soul. And it was perhaps with reference to this that the prophetic and perfected soul declared: 'I opened my mouth and drew breath.'

"And let us understand that by the 'mouth' of the Bridegroom is meant the power by which he enlightens the mind and, as by some word of love addressed to her — if so she deserves to experience the presence of power so great — makes plain whatever is unknown and dark to her. And this is the truer, closer, holier kiss, which is said to be granted by the Bridegroom-Word of God to the Bride — that is to say, to the pure and perfect soul; it is of this happening that the kiss, which we give to one another in church at the holy mysteries, is a figure.

"As often, therefore, as we find some problem pertaining to the divine teachings and meanings revealed in our hearts without instructors' help, so often may we believe that kisses have been given to us by the Bridegroom-Word of God. But, when we seek the meaning of something of this sort and cannot find it, then let us make this prayer our own and beg from God the visitation of his Word, saying, 'Let him kiss me with the kisses of his mouth.' For the Father knows each single soul's capacity and understands the right time for a soul to receive the kisses of the Word in lights and insights of this sort."

ABBREVIATIONS

OLD TESTAMENT

Genesis	Gn	Nehemiah	Ne	Baruch	Ba
Exodus	Ex	Tobit	Tb	Ezekiel	Ezk
Leviticus	Lv	Judith	Jdt	Daniel	Dn
Numbers	Nb	Esther	Est	Hosea	Ho
Deuteronomy	Dt	1 Maccabees	1 M	Joel	Jl
Joshua	Jos	2 Maccabees	2 M	Amos	Am
Judges	Jg	Job	Jb	Obadiah	Ob
Ruth	Rt	Psalms	Ps	Jonah	Jon
1 Samuel	1 S	Proverbs	Pr	Micah	Mi
2 Samuel	2 S	Ecclesiastes	Ec	Nahum	Na
1 Kings	1 K	Song of Songs	Sg	Habakkuk	Hab
2 Kings	2 K	Wisdom	Ws	Zephaniah	Zp
1 Chronicles	1 Ch	Sirach	Si	Haggai	Hg
2 Chronicles	2 Ch	Isaiah	Is	Malachi	Ml
Ezra	Ezr	Jeremiah	Jr	Zechariah	Zc
		Lamentations	Lm		

NEW TESTAMENT

Matthew	Mt	Ephesians	Ep	Hebrews	Heb
Mark	Mk	Philippians	Ph	James	Jm
Luke	Lk	Colossians	Col	1 Peter	1 P
John	Jn	1 Thessalonians	1 Th	2 Peter	2 P
Acts	Ac	2 Thessalonians	2 Th	1 John	1 Jn
Romans	Rm	1 Timothy	1 Tm	2 John	2 Jn
1 Corinthians	1 Cor	2 Timothy	2 Tm	3 John	3 Jn
2 Corinthians	2 Cor	Titus	Tt	Jude	Jude
Galatians	Gal	Philemon	Phm	Revelation	Rv

CHAPTER ONE

CHAPTER ONE

"After Six Days. . ."

Scripture As An Epiphany Of Christ

THE HEART of our faith about the Scriptures is that in them God speaks to us. "Thus says the Lord" is the awesome truth of every line. As Christians we believe that this same God "who in the past spoke to our forefathers through the prophets at many times and in various ways, in these last days has spoken to us by his Son" (Heb 1:1-2). "In the beginning was the Word. . . and the Word became flesh and dwelt among us" (Jn 1:1,14). The Father's revelation on Tabor — "This is my beloved Son; listen to him" (Mk 9:7) — is the key to every line of Scripture. In every line it is this eternal Word of God who is speaking to us.

Just ask yourself: Whenever you open the Bible, or hear it read, are you aware that you are speaking with Christ himself? What a profound dignity and gift to be addressed by Christ! In one of his beautiful commentaries on the Scriptures Jesus says, "They are called 'gods' to whom the word of God is addressed" (Jn 10:35). What a sublime privilege is ours! Out of his boundless freedom and love God has chosen to speak to us and not keep silent.

The Bible, then, is Christ speaking to us. I will be using the accounts of the Transfiguration * as the model for our approaching and encountering Christ in the Scriptures. I have found in these accounts most of the attitudes necessary for allowing the Word to dwell within us.

There can be little doubt that the Transfiguration was an

---

* For convenience, the three accounts of the Transfiguration are presented in Appendix A.

extremely important and significant event for the disciples. It is recounted in all three Synoptic Gospels — Matthew 17:1-8, Mark 9:2-8 and Luke 9:28-36; there is also the beautiful account in 2 Peter 1:16-19:

> We did not follow cleverly invented stories when we told you about the power and coming of our Lord Jesus Christ, but we were eyewitnesses of his majesty. For he received honor and glory from God the Father when the voice came to him from the Majestic Glory, saying, "This is my Son, whom I love; with him I am well pleased." We ourselves heard this voice that came from heaven when we were with him on the sacred mountain. And we have heard the word of the prophets made more certain, and you will do well to pay attention to it, as to a light shining in a dark place, until the day dawns and the morning star rises in your hearts.

Both Matthew and Mark begin their accounts of the Transfiguration with the phrase, "After six days. . ."; Luke has, "Now about eight days after. . ." The reference is clearly to Exodus 24:15-18:

> When Moses went up on the mountain, the cloud covered it, and the glory of the Lord settled on Mount Sinai. For six days the cloud covered the mountain, and *on the seventh day* the Lord called to Moses from within the cloud. To the Israelites the glory of the Lord looked like a consuming fire on top of the mountain. Then Moses entered the cloud as he went on up the mountain. And he stayed on the mountain forty days and forty nights.

Surely one of the most important aspects of this scene is what is related further on in Exodus: "The Lord would speak to Moses face to face, as a man speaks with his friend"

(Ex 33:11). Once again now, on Tabor, the all-holy God in the person of Christ, is speaking face to face with his friends. And this is the heart of the mystery of Scripture for us now: Christ speaking face to face with us, his friends. "I no longer call you servants, but my friends," and thus he makes known to us, through this conversation, everything he has learned from his Father (Jn 15:15).

"Theophany" means the appearance or manifestation of God. Much of the Bible concerns encounters of various people with God. The many references to the "face of God" surely mean encountering him as a living Person. Such a meeting ought to engage our whole being. According to the guidance of the Spirit this encounter will now take on the awesomeness of Sinai, now the struggle of Jacob, now the repentance of David, now the quiet sitting of Mary, the sister of Martha, at the feet of Jesus.

It is this speaking face to face with Christ which constitutes the essence, and deepens the reality of, *personhood*. A person is someone who is capable of speaking with God. Jesus calls such persons "gods," in the passage quoted earlier. Listening to and speaking with God is the most lifegiving act of which we are capable. What an unparalleled gift, then, to have in a Book the very words of God!

A brief word here about our use and handling of the Bible itself.

Praise God that now in many of our churches the Scriptures are prominently displayed! In the Eastern rites the Gospel Book is often encased in a splendid binding of real gold and silver. It is carried in solemn procession and, because it is Christ himself, can only be placed on the altar, which is the throne of God. Many saints would never read the Scriptures except on their knees.

It is good that the Bible is carried around by many people, but we must strive to acquire a permanent sacramental reverence for the Book of the Scriptures, and not simply a reverence confined to the liturgical setting. If we must carry the Bible with us, let us carry it as we would carry the Blessed Sacrament to the sick, since we believe Christ is just as present in his Word.

The presence of Christ, God speaking to us — these realities of faith must predominate whenever we read, use, or approach the Scriptures in any way. Even when the emphasis is on study, we must remember that we are not so much acquiring ideas *about* God as seeking to allow ourselves to be more totally grasped by his presence, seeking to allow his Face to shine on us, desiring that his Word dwell more within us so that we might carry out his will in history. The Bible has been given to us not for information but for *transformation* into Christ. It is God's Word to draw us into communion with him.

My main theme, then, is this: Using the accounts of the Transfiguration I will develop the scriptural attitudes necessary for our encounter with Christ. Through this dialogue, Christ wishes to transform us into "gods", giving us the dignity of those who are addressed by God. Unlike Moses, our faces now are unveiled through the gift of the Holy Spirit. "We, with unveiled faces, all contemplate the Lord's glory . . . being transformed into his likeness with ever-increasing glory, which comes from the Lord, who is the Spirit" (2 Cor 3:18).

Origen

Exodus Homily XIII FC

"*I wish to admonish you with examples from your religious practices. You who are accustomed to take part in divine mysteries know, when you receive the body of the Lord, how you protect it with all caution and veneration lest any small part fall from it, lest anything of the consecrated gift be lost. For you believe, and correctly, that you are answerable if anything falls from there by neglect. But if you are so careful to preserve his body, and rightly so, how do you think that there is less guilt to have neglected God's word than to have neglected his body?*"

CHAPTER TWO

CHAPTER TWO

"Jesus Took With Him..."

Scripture As Daily Intimate Conversation With Christ

WHEN I SAY I will be using the accounts of the Transfiguration to describe the necessary faith attitudes for encountering Christ in the Scriptures, I am not implying that our every encounter should or will be the dazzling and overpowering experience of Tabor. Sometimes it may be. But even for the apostles, this experience on Tabor was extraordinary. I will use the expression, "Jesus took with him," to refer to our daily, often quite ordinary, meetings with Christ, even though on this one occasion he took them to Tabor.

Jesus spent much more time walking and talking privately with his disciples than he did preaching to the crowds. The Gospels often tell us that he explained privately to his disciples what he had spoken publicly (Lk 8:9f). I think our daily Scripture reading is more like that.

We are sitting with Jesus on a hillside. He has just taken a little snooze. As we listen to him, he may put a question to us as he often did to the disciples: "Who do you say that I am?" Or we may ask him the meaning of the parables, or of some of his other words. For after the truth that the Scriptures are God speaking to us, the next most important truth is that only the Spirit of God can explain these words to us: "The Paraclete, the Holy Spirit whom the Father will send in my

name, will instruct you in everything, and remind you of all
that I told you" (Jn 14:26). This too is a constant teaching of
the Bible:

> How different the man who devotes himself
> to the study of the law of the Most High. . .
> His care is to seek the Lord, his Maker,
> to petition the Most High,
> To open his lips in prayer,
> to ask pardon for his sins.
> Then, if it pleases the Lord Almighty,
> he will be filled with the spirit of understanding;
> He will pour forth his words of wisdom,
> and in prayer give thanks to the Lord,
> Who will direct his knowledge and his counsel,
> as he meditates upon his mysteries.   Si 39:1, 6-7

> By your light we see light.   Ps 36:10

> Send forth your light and your truth.
> Let these be my guide to lead me to your holy mountain,
> and to the place where you dwell.   Ps 43:3

> And so I prayed and understanding was given to me.
> I entered and the spirit of Wisdom came to me.   Ws 7:7

> All wisdom comes from the Lord and with him
> it remains forever.   Si 1:1

Only God can explain God. "No one knows the thoughts
of God except the Spirit of God" (1 Cor 2:11). And we have
received "the Spirit who is from God, that we may understand what God has freely given us. . . This is what we speak
. . . words taught by the Spirit, expressing spiritual truths in
spiritual words" (12-13).

The episode of Jesus explaining the Scriptures to the disciples along the road to Emmaus says it exactly (Lk 24:25-27, 32). This "burning within the heart" as the Word is being explained by the Word, is the fulfillment of God's purpose in giving us the Scriptures. The burning is the fire of the Spirit cauterizing our heart of stone, turning it into a heart of flesh.

The good news is that this burning of the heart, as Jesus explains the Scriptures to us, is available to us every day, provided we have the faith dispositions of the heart.

As the disciples came down from the mount of the Transfiguration they had the courage to ask Jesus questions about what they had seen. We too must have the courage to ask. We are often like the disciples when Jesus told them he would be handed over into the power of men. They did not understand and were afraid to ask (Mk 9:32). If we daily approach Jesus, and with faith and courage ask him what his words mean, he will tell us. Only *he* can really explain them.

This is our true life: having our hearts burn within us (Lk 24:32); having our minds opened by Jesus so we can understand the Scriptures (Lk 24:45); knowing our Master's business (Jn 15:15); being able to bear all that Jesus wishes to speak to us (Jn 16:12); hearing Jesus speak to us plainly about the Father (Jn 16:25); understanding that Jesus knows all things (Jn 16:30).

May I introduce Our Lady here? Already in the 3rd century Origen said that in order to understand the Scriptures you must lean on the breast of Jesus and have Mary for your Mother. Again, this is not "piety." It expresses the profundity of how the divine mysteries are communicated to us.

Tradition is unanimous in acclaiming John (the Divine, the Theologian) and his Gospel as the most sublime. Is this not because he leaned on the Lord's breast and loved him more? And Mary's greatness? Is it not because she perfectly believed "that what the Lord had said to her will be accomplished" (Lk 1:15)? She is doubly blessed because she nurtured Christ in her womb and on her breasts, and heard the Word of God and kept it (Lk 11:27-28).

Mary also treasured up all the words and events of the life of Christ and "pondered them in her heart" (Lk 2:19). Did you ever consider that in Mary's heart are thousands of words spoken by Christ that have not been recorded for us? Not only that: as the person who knows and loves Christ most of all, she more than anyone else can help us understand the mysteries of his life and words. Devotion to her is also one of the keys for understanding the words of Christ.

Origen

Commentary on John SF 107

"*No one has revealed his divinity as John. . . One can even dare to say that the gospels are the first fruits of all the scriptures, but that John is the first fruits of the gospels. No one can grasp its meaning who has not lain on Jesus' breast and [like John] also received Mary from Jesus as one's own mother. So great must one be who is to become another John in order, like John, to be shown Jesus by Jesus.*

"*For if Mary has no other son but Jesus, . . . but Jesus says to his mother: 'Behold your son' (Jn 19:26), and not: 'Behold, this too is your son,' it is the same as saying: 'Behold, this is Jesus to whom you gave birth.' For everyone who has come to perfection 'lives no longer,' but 'Christ lives' in him. And because Christ lives in him, it is said of him to Mary: 'Behold your son,' Christ.*

"*How elevated a mind we must have in order to be able to perceive worthily this WORD lying hidden within the earthen treasures of the ordinary word. . . !*"

CHAPTER THREE

"Peter, James And John. . ."

Hearing The Word As Members Of The Church

I SEE THE PRIVILEGED GROUP of three — Peter, James and John — as a symbol for two dimensions at the heart of hearing the Word of God: (1) Hearing together in the liturgical assembly where Christ can speak the same word to all, and (2) Hearing the Word as a member of a Body, allowing our consciousness of membership in that Body to condition and affect our hearing.

Because we are "a chosen race, a royal priesthood, a holy nation, God's own people" (1 P 2:9), and, as Christians, members of Christ Body, the liturgy is the primary place to hear the Word. In the Old Testament, the people were brought together precisely to hear the Word of God *as a people*, so that they could all respond together, "Amen! Amen!" (Ne 8:6). This communal hearing is what actually made them a people. Just as personality in its essence is speaking with and responding to God, so a people is created by all responding together to the Lord. They agreed *together* to obey his Word.

The most ancient Christian meaning of the word "mystical" referred to the encounter with Christ in the liturgy — in the Eucharist and in the Scriptures (Louis Bouyer). Only secondarily, and much later historically, does it refer to private encounters with God. (Most people in the modern world probably give it this latter meaning.)

What I am speaking about in this book, even when referring to the direct teaching of the Spirit, is not *private* interpretation of the Word in the sense of an isolated individual. What I mean is *personal* appropriation and assimilation. The Christian never listens to Christ as an isolated individual, although he or she may physically be alone. "Peter, James and John" are symbolic of the communal setting of the liturgy in which the Scriptures are primarily heard.

They are also symbolic of an "ecclesial mind." The Bible is a family book, a book of a people. We always read such a book with a communal consciousness — that is, with the understanding of a family member.

Even the statements in the New Testament about being taught directly by the Holy Spirit refer first of all to the Church, to the Body, to the community. The "you" in the following passages are all in the *plural*:

> I have much more to say to you, more than you can now bear. But when he, the Spirit of truth, comes, he will guide you into all truth.   Jn 16:12

> But you have an anointing from the Holy One, and all of you know the truth . . . the anointing you received from him remains in you, and you do not need anyone to teach you. But his anointing teaches you about all things. . .
> 1 Jn 2:20, 27

A misunderstanding of these and similar passages can confuse *direct* guidance by the Holy Spirit with *isolated* guidance.

The proper perspective is that *the Holy Spirit speaks to me directly as a member of the Church.* To emphasize the Church's role to the point of *substitution* for personal inspiration, or to emphasize the personal (in an individualistic sense) to the detriment of the Church's guidance, are both harmful aberrations. What we have on Tabor is Jesus speaking personally to apostles as members of the Church.

The Acts of the Apostles shows that Scripture interpretation is not a private affair in the story of Philip and the Ethiopian eunuch (Ac 8:26-40). Through a private revelation, Philip is led to the Ethiopian, who is reading aloud from Isaiah. "Do you understand what you are reading?" Philip asked the Ethiopian. "How can I understand unless someone explains it to me?" he replied.

This is the ancient Catholic understanding: without the Church's mind we cannot understand what is said to us privately. This does not mean that we cannot have a *personal* relationship with Christ in the Scriptures. What it means is that we cannot have a *private, isolated* relationship with him. We are members of one another, and we need one another to understand the full import of the Lord's speaking to us. In the New Testament there are no isolated Christians or communities. All are members, one of another. We always meet Christ in the Scriptures, therefore, *with* "Peter, James and John."

Origen

Commentary on the Song of Songs
SF 109

"But when 'the veil is taken away' from the spouse, namely, the church 'turned to the Lord' (2 Cor 3:14, 16), she suddenly sees him 'leaping over' those 'mountains,' namely, the books of the law, and not so much appearing as, because of his open and clear manifestation, 'bounding over the hills' (Sg 2:8) of the prophetic books. It is as if she, paging through the sheets of the prophetic reading, finds Christ 'bounding' out of them and in each passage in the readings, now that the 'veil' which first covered them is 'taken away,' sees him emerge and spring forth and break out in an unmistakable appearance."

CHAPTER FOUR

CHAPTER FOUR

"Led Them Up A High Mountain Apart By Themselves"

Encountering Christ Alone

HEARING THE WORD OF CHRIST in the liturgical assembly is absolutely essential, since we are not only separate individuals but more importantly members of his Body. But much of our dialogue with Christ does and even should take place alone.

Most of the encounters of people with God in the Bible occur when they are alone. Abraham at the oak of Mamre, Jacob's wrestling with the angel, Moses at the burning bush, the visions of the prophets — all take place alone with God.

We could probably come up with many sophisticated reasons why this should be so. It suffices here to say that God is the great Lover, and lovers seek silence and solitude with their beloved. And it is a fact that many of our most personal experiences of God happen when we are alone.

Scripture tells us that the Lord Jesus himself often sought out solitary places in the hills to pray: "spent the whole night in prayer to God," "arose early in the morning and went out to pray." I presume he did this all his life and not only during his public ministry. He who was "one with the Father," he who was never alone "because the Father is always with me," he who didn't have to struggle to achieve a balance between action and contemplation(!), he who didn't *need* to separate himself from distractions in order to commune with the Father, he, the Incarnate Word, often went apart to pray.

Why did he do this? It was not simply "as an example" for us. He did it because he was fully human. Going apart to pray is not a part of our human weakness, to be superceded when we are fully spiritually mature. Going apart to be alone with God, to commune with the Beloved in solitude, is part of being fully human. That's why Jesus did it.

Without attempting, then, to give a proof, I state that going apart by oneself is one of the best ways to hear the voice of the Beloved. This practice is consonant with the lives of all the saints, the witness of the Lord and the Scriptures, and the testimony of all those who have ever tasted the delights of intimate conversation with God in solitude and silence.

Nor is it a matter of "being able to think better and collect one's thoughts." *Silence allows another Voice to be heard.* This is not the voice of self-analysis, not the voice of interior turmoil or profound thoughts. It is the Voice transcending our own voices, the Voice of the Beloved, the Voice of God.

Thus, while it is true that the actual, communal hearing of the Word is vital (and that small Bible groups have their place and value), we are also called to daily go apart and sit at the feet of the Lord and listen to his voice in silence. One of the translations of Elijah's encounter with God at the entrance of the cave is, "After the fire, the sound of utter silence" (1 K 19:1-13; cf. vs. 12).

There is the heart-rending story of Hagar fleeing from Sarai into the desert. The angel consoles her with the prediction of the birth of Ishmael. "She gave this name to the Lord who spoke to her: 'You are the God who sees me,' for she said, 'I have now seen the One who sees me' " (Gn 16:13). Like Hagar, each one of us will have our own personal name for the Beloved, which is the way we experience him in our love-making.

A great spiritual classic of our time is Catherine de Hueck Doherty's *Poustinia.** It is a profound call (which many in our day have heeded) to go apart with the Scriptures only and commune with God in solitude. Many people are creating little "mountain tops" in their basements or attics, or setting aside some part of their room or home, creating definite places where they can daily listen to Christ's voice alone. Jesus took Peter, James and John up a high mountain away from the crowds. Part of our normal, daily encounter with Christ in the Scriptures should take place in silence and quiet.

When they came down from the mountain "Jesus commanded them, 'Tell no one the vision. . .' " Lovers have secrets. The Lord desires to speak secrets into your heart which cannot be found in any commentary or heard in any classroom or study course. One Lent I decided to read Origen's commentary on the Song of Songs. As I settled down to read I got no further than the first few lines and the Lord said to me: "This is what I said to Origen. I could say more personal things to you if you believed in my presence." So I put the commentary away and allowed the Beloved to speak to me himself.

* Ave Maria Press, Notre Dame, Indiana, 1975.

Origen

Commentary on Matthew   ANF

"The garments of Jesus are the expressions and letters of the Gospels with which He has clothed Himself. These become white to those who go up into the high mountain along with Jesus."

CHAPTER FIVE

CHAPTER FIVE

"... To Pray. And As He Was Praying..."

Praying The Scriptures

JESUS WENT UP TABOR to pray. It was as he was praying that he was transfigured.

I quoted earlier from Sirach that as one prayerfully approaches the study of the Lord's Word, "Then, if it pleases the Lord Almighty, he will be filled with the spirit of understanding" (Si 39:6).

The Bible is not just another book: it is an incarnation of Christ. Ideally, every time we open or approach it — if only to look up a reference — we should pause and realize that we are approaching God. The Scriptures should always be approached as a Person, and, at least interiorly, we should always be on our knees. If a Person, then we are entering into a conversation; and conversation with God is prayer. In short, we should always be praying the Scriptures.

I would like to describe for you, in a few simple words, the most ancient and basic way of Christian prayer. It is praying from the Scriptures. This was the way of the early Christians, of the desert fathers, of all the great teaching Fathers of the Church. All the saints eventually were led along this same way. In one sense, there is no better way for Christians to pray.

It is important to always remember that God initiates

prayer. Because of a lack of spiritual awareness we believe that we take the initiative. Not really. Frequently in the Gospel, Jesus summons people into his presence. (Concerning the blind Bartimaeus Jesus said, "Call him" [Mk 10:49].) Even when people rush up to Jesus without this visible summons, it is the Spirit of Jesus himself moving people to approach him. So whenever we open the Scriptures we should pause for a few moments and realize that the King is summoning us into his presence out of his great mercy and graciousness.

Then we open (let's say) the Gospel text and read. This is the Lord himself speaking to us in his own words. They are not time-conditioned ("Heaven and earth will pass away, but my words will never pass away" [Mk 13:31]), nor are they meant only for a select few ("He who has ears to hear, let him hear" [Mk 4:9]). They are the eternal Word speaking the heart's self-understanding to itself. In the light of these words of Christ we understand who God is, his plan for us and the world, what he is asking of us. This is what tradition calls *lectio divina*, godly reading.

After Christ himself has spoken to us, we pause in silence, reflect on his words, and allow them to penetrate into our heart like rain soaking into the ground. It is the time for interior pondering, or what tradition calls *meditation*.

Having reflected, we then reply to Christ in our own words, thanking him, praising him, petitioning him for what we need. This is prayer, properly speaking.

Finally, because we have been in dialogue with the Beloved we pause again in silence, savoring the wonder of his love. This is contemplation — the silent resting in the arms of Christ.

These four acts, or phases, of our encounter with God contain all the movements of what is generally known as prayer. Let us take an example.

By his Spirit Jesus summons us into his presence: "Call him." We approach in reverence and Jesus says, "Unless you become like little children you cannot enter the kingdom of heaven." This is eternal Wisdom speaking to you. We are in amazement that we are "sharers in the divine nature," are "gods," privileged to speak with God. We ponder: what does this mean? What is this childlikeness of which he is speaking? Does he mean to be simple? Open? Totally dependent upon his Father as he is?

Then you pray. "Lord, I know my heart is far from being childlike, far from being simple. You had an absolute simplicity and harmony in all your actions. You were totally dependent on your Father in all things, the perfect Child. Help me to be childlike in the depths of my heart."

Then you are quiet once more as you allow the presence of the Person to whom you are speaking to envelop your whole being. Without words, you simply bask in the warmth of his Face, realizing, like Hagar, that he *sees* you in your poverty and need. That he will come is as sure as the dawn, since he delights in those who wait for his love.

The perfect example in the Bible of how to approach Jesus is Mary, Martha's sister. She was in loving awe of Jesus. By his attractiveness he drew her to him. She came and sat silently at his feet, her heart yearning to be filled with his life-giving words. This attentiveness was the center of her life, the one "really necessary thing" for her. She became absorbed in the contemplation of his beauty (cf. Lk 10:38-42).

We do not always approach Jesus like that. Sometimes we are like Nicodemus who approached out of curiosity. We do not pray and listen but carry on a discussion! Or worse, we are like the Pharisees who criticize and dispute his words as one debater with another!

No. In the Scriptures we are approaching our Lord and

our God, to hear his Word, to pour out our hearts to him, to seek his grace, and to rest in his presence. Jesus took Peter, James and John up a high mountain *to pray*. You too, when you open the Scriptures, must *pray*, since it is a meeting with God.

Origen

Commentary on Matthew   ANF

"Perhaps it is possible to see the Word Transfigured before us if we have seen the absolute Word holding converse with the Father, and we pray to him for such things as the true High-Priest might pray for to the only true God."

CHAPTER SIX

"He Was Transfigured Before Them, And His Face Shone Like The Sun, And His Garments Became White As Light"

Meeting The Glorious Christ In The Scriptures

WHATEVER symbolic or allegorical interpretation may be given to the Transfiguration, its simple and obvious meaning is that, as much as they could bear, the disciples were given a vision of the majesty and splendor of Christ.

During most of his earthly life Jesus veiled his glory. Taking the form of a servant (Ph 2:7), part of his "not clinging to God's prerogatives" (Ph 2:6) was to prevent the splendor of his divinity from dazzling our eyes. (Who, then, could *not* believe?) Here on earth we are called to live by faith. But for a brief moment on Tabor Jesus allowed something of the brilliance of his divinity to burst forth.

When Paul says that he no longer regards Christ "in terms of mere human judgment" (2 Cor 5:16), what he means is that he no longer thinks of Christ merely as an historical person who was crucified and is now dead. Along the road to Damascus Paul met the living, risen, glorious Christ.

Listen to Paul's account of this vision in Acts 26:13-18

where he is talking to King Agrippa. There are certain features of this particular account relevant to our topic:

> About noon, O King, as I was on the road, I saw a light from heaven, brighter than the sun, blazing around me and my companions. We all fell to the ground, and I heard a voice saying to me in Aramaic, "Saul, Saul, why do you persecute me? It is hard for you to kick against the goad."
>
> Then I asked, "Who are you, Lord?" "I am Jesus, whom you are persecuting," the Lord replied. "Now get up and stand on your feet. I have appeared to you to appoint you as a servant and as a witness of what you have seen of me and what I will show you. I will rescue you from your own people and from the Gentiles. I am sending you to them to open their eyes and turn them from darkness to light, and from the power of Satan to God, so that they may receive forgiveness of sins and a place among those who are sanctified by faith in me."

This is the longest speech of the risen Christ in the Scriptures. This epiphany has features similar to the Transfiguration — a light from heaven brighter than the sun, the falling to the ground, a heavenly voice — in short, an overwhelming experience of the glorious Christ. The Christ to whom Paul was related ever after was this glorious, risen Christ of the Damascus road.

So too with us: the Christ with whom we are speaking now in prayer, or whenever we open the Scriptures, is this glorious Christ. Jesus is now and forever risen and in glory at the Father's right hand. What we must always remember is that whenever we open the Scriptures we are conversing with the glorious Christ.

If you are meditating on the passage where Christ heals

the daughter of Jairus (Mk 5:21-24, 35-43), your consciousness can no longer be that of Jairus, or of his wife, or of one
of the apostles who was present. The raising of this little girl
happens now for us against the background of the glorious
Christ. Her raising is a faint reflection of the great act of God
in raising Christ from the dead; a symbol also of our own
resurrection which will occur through our own faith in the
risen Christ.

The same for the Old Testament. As Abraham walks up
the mountain with a heavy heart, we know not only that his
son will be spared (Gn 22:1-19). We know that Abraham is a
faint reflection of God the Father who did not spare his
only-begotten Son for the life of the world. Even more: we
know that this Son (who was not spared like Isaac) is now
glorified with the Father because of obedience.

If you read the songs of the Suffering Servant in Isaiah,
those pains are already radiant in the glorified Christ. When
we read the passion narratives of the Gospels, we know the
end of the story: Christ is now risen and glorified with the
Father.

Jesus, as God, was always the most glorious One, even
before his passion and death, since he and the Father were
always one. Christ allowed his humanity to veil this glory
during most of his lifetime. But on one occasion — the
Transfiguration — he allowed that glory to shine through.
Tabor was a revelation — a drawing back of the veil — of
who Jesus really was. You might say it was a "preview of
coming attractions"! It is this glorious Christ who now
speaks to us on every page of the Scriptures. The Holy Spirit
will enlighten you so that each word is illuminated by his
radiant presence.

Finally, read again what Jesus said to Saul in the passage
from Acts quoted above. It is a wonderful summary of what
the glorious Christ now calls each of us to do.

Origen

Commentary on John   SF 109

"For truly, before Jesus, the scripture was water, but after Jesus it has become wine for us."

CHAPTER SEVEN

"And Behold Two Men Talked With Him, Moses And Elijah"

The Whole Of Scripture Is Only One Word: Christ

One day in the synagogue Jesus stood up to read from Isaiah. Then he rolled up the scroll and sat down. He said: "Today this scripture passage is fulfilled in your hearing" (Lk 4:21).

And in the beautiful encounter on the road to Emmaus, after his resurrection, beginning with Moses and all the prophets, Jesus explained to those two dejected disciples "what was said in all the Scriptures concerning himself" (Lk 24:27).

Jesus talking with Moses and Elijah on Tabor is a symbol of this truth: Every line of Scripture is ultimately about Christ. There is only one Word, Christ. Every other word is an expression of this one Word and points to him. This is the great key to the Scriptures.

Origen begins his commentary on the Book of Genesis by sounding this great harmonic line, which he then plays throughout all his commentaries:

"In the beginning God made heaven and earth" (Gn 1:1).
What is the beginning of all things except our Lord and Savior of all, Jesus Christ, the first-born of every creature?

In this beginning, therefore, that is, in his Word, God made
heaven and earth. FC 47

Just as every creature was made "in him" and is a reflection of the first-born of the Father, so Scripture is a reflection of this one Word, Christ. There is only one Word, just as
there is only one Gospel. We have several expressions of the
Word in four Gospels, but there is only one Gospel, Christ.

On Tabor, Jesus was explaining to Moses and Elijah how
everything in their lives and ministries were about him.
*Christ is the meaning of everything Moses and Elijah ever said and
did.* Christ is the real meaning of Scripture, and this meaning is revealed to each believer through the Holy Spirit.

I am going to show you something. As I write this I am
going to open the Scriptures at random and demonstrate
what I have just said. I opened to this line from Isaiah
(29:22-24):

> No longer will Jacob be ashamed;
> no longer will their faces grow pale.
> When they see among them their children,
> the work of my hands,
> they will keep my name holy;
> they will acknowledge the holiness of
> the Holy One of Jacob,
> and will stand in awe of the God of Israel.
> Those who are wayward in spirit
> will gain understanding;
> those who complain
> will accept instruction.

What is the "real" meaning of this passage? Jacob is the
whole human race — you and me — ashamed and dejected.
Jesus comes along, as he did on the road to Emmaus, and
cheers us up. It is from him that we, who were wayward in

spirit because of our sins, gain true understanding and instruction. Who better than Jesus showed us how to ac-knowledge the holiness of God, how to stand in awe of the God of Israel?

You see? This is not a distortion of the text or a "pious" interpretation. It is not the *only* meaning of the text — the Holy Spirit shows different facets of Christ's glory to differ-ent people, and a strict exegesis of this passage would bring up other valuable points as well. But this "allegorical" in-terpretation is valid as well. With faith in the glorified Christ, and surrounded by the company of the Church, the deepest mysteries of this text are available to us — for "the mystery is Christ in you."

The second truth about Jesus speaking with Moses and Elijah on Tabor is that, not only are the Scriptures *about* Jesus, but that *Jesus himself, as the Word, was the Word speaking through them.*

There is only one Spirit of God which spoke through Moses and all the prophets: the Spirit of Jesus. There is no other. The Gospel is simply the ultimate expression of the Spirit speaking in the now-Incarnate Word. The Spirit in Moses and Elijah and Daniel and Matthew and Paul is the Spirit of Jesus, and it is now the glorified Christ who speaks to us through them all.

Origen again: "You are to understand [all of the] Scriptures in this way: as the one, perfect body of the Word." Every line of the Bible, no matter who spoke it or *how it came about*, was spoken by the Spirit of Jesus.

This is a very consoling truth. Regardless of what the actual words of Christ were, regardless of what lines in John's Gospel are actually a "meditation" of the evangelist, regardless of the different versions of Jesus's sayings and parables found in the different Gospels, all are ultimately inspired by the Spirit of Christ.

I believe God meant all his children to be able to approach the Scriptures and understand the essential message. But God's Word must be approached in faith, with the attitudes I am here describing. (These attitudes themselves are in the Scriptures and the Spirit leads people of good faith to them.) The core truth is this: "These Scriptures testify about me" (Jn 5:39). With this faith, and with the guidance of the Church in essentials, anyone of good heart can learn from the Scriptures what is necessary for his or her deep life with God. Jesus himself, through his Spirit, will explain them to you, just as he explained them to Moses and Elijah on Tabor.

Origen

Commentary on Exodus   SF 100-101

"Paul says somewhere in writing to the Corinthians: 'For we know that our fathers were all under the cloud, and all were baptized into Moses in the cloud and in the sea, and all ate the same supernatural food and all drank the same supernatural drink. For they drank from the supernatural Rock, which followed them, and the Rock was Christ' (1 Cor 10:1-4). You can see how different Paul's tradition is from the historical reading: what the Jews think is a crossing of the sea, Paul calls baptism; where they see a cloud, Paul puts the Holy Spirit; and it is in this way that he wants us to understand what the Lord commanded in the Gospels when he said: 'Whoever is not born again of water and the Holy Spirit cannot enter into the kingdom of heaven' (Jn 3:5). And the manna too, which the Jews think of as food for the stomach and satisfaction for hunger, Paul calls 'spiritual food' (1 Cor 10:3). And not just Paul, but the Lord too, says in the same Gospel: 'Your fathers ate the manna in the wilderness, and they died. Whoever eats of the bread which I give him will not die forever' (Jn 6:49, 50). And right after that: 'I am the bread which came down from heaven' (Jn 6:51). Hence Paul speaks quite openly about 'the rock which followed them': 'And the Rock was Christ' (1 Cor 10:4).

How then are we to act, who have received such principles of interpretation from Paul, the teacher of the Church? Does it not seem right that such a method coming to us from the tradition should serve as a model in all other instances? Or shall we, as some would like, abandon what so great and holy an apostle has given us and turn back to 'Jewish myths' (Tt 1:14)? I, at least, if I am interpreting this differently than Paul, think that in this I am extending my hands to the enemies of Christ, and that this is what the prophet says: 'Woe to him who gives his neighbor to drink from the turmoil of confusion' (Hab 2:15)."

CHAPTER EIGHT

"They Were Talking About His Exodus"

Scripture As Exodus Into Christ

Why DO WE CONVERSE with Christ in the Scriptures? Or rather, why *should* we converse with him? For the same reason that he became incarnate and spoke to us, so that we might pass over into his divine life and be saved: "I have come that they may have life" (Jn 10:10); "I have heard them crying out because of their slave drivers, and I am ` concerned about their suffering. So I have come down to rescue them. . ." (Ex 3:7-8); "I have waited, waited for the Lord, and he stooped toward me and heard my cry. He drew me out of the pit of destruction" (Ps 40:2-3). All throughout the Scriptures God's people cry out to be saved, and God comes to save them. This saving cannot occur without a passing over from our old, sinful life to new life.

If you read the Scriptures without anything changing in your heart and life, you have not really encountered the living, glorious Christ. You surely have not allowed the Word to dwell within you. The "mystery" that Christ was speaking about with Moses and Elijah on Tabor was about "his *exodos* [death/passing/exodus/departure] which he was to accomplish in Jerusalem" (Lk 9:31).

The deepest meaning of the word "mystery" is that it is a sacred action, a sacred drama, through which we are drawn into God. It is not (as regards the Scriptures) trying to figure out the meaning of a text. Even if our meditation begins there, our conversation with Christ is not complete unless we allow the power of that meaning to draw us more deeply into the life of Christ. Christ himself is the Sacred Act of God, the Mystery par excellence, as St. Paul so often says. There is no real knowledge of him without a passing over.

For the Christian, true knowledge of God comes from loving him — "We know that we have come to know him if we obey his commands" (1 Jn 2:3) — but there is no growth in love without a passing over — "If anyone would be a follower of mine let him deny himself and take up his cross" (Lk 9:23). The writings of the saints have such wisdom and power precisely because of this: through love, through dying with Christ, they "see" God and the things of God. "I have more understanding than the elders, for I *obey* your precepts" (Ps 119:100).

Remember that one day some Greeks came and said to one of the disciples, "We want to see Jesus" (Jn 12:21). Why did they want to see him? What did Jesus say on that occasion in their hearing? He knew they were seeking for wisdom, so he told them how to get it: "I tell you the truth, unless a kernel of wheat falls to the ground and dies, it remains only a single seed. But if it dies it produces many seeds. The man who loves his life will lose it, while the man who hates his life in this world will keep it for eternal life" (Jn 12:24-25).

Did they "get it"? Did they understand that "the wisdom of this world is foolishness in God's sight" (1 Cor 3:19)? Did they understand that true wisdom and knowledge comes from dying to sin and rising to goodness?

Reflect on almost every encounter of Christ with people in the Gospels. Read the parables. They are all calls to pass over from apathy to caring, from sluggishness to vigilance, from unrepentance to repentance. What Jesus asked the people about John the Baptist (Lk 7:24-26) we could ask about people opening the Scriptures: "When you opened the Gospels, what did you expect to hear? A Christ confirming all your illusions? No, I tell you. But what did you expect to hear? A Christ calling you to relinquish your pride, your selfishness, your mediocrity? Yes, and more than that: your very self!"

"Not everyone who says to me 'Lord, Lord' will enter the kingdom of heaven, but only he who does the will of my Father" (Mt 7:21). Not everyone who merely opens the Gospels and reads will be approved by the Lord: "Everyone who hears these words of mine and does not put them into practice is like a foolish man. . ." (Mt 7:26). Foolishness comes from *hearing without doing*; wisdom comes from *entering the kingdom*, passing over from darkness to light — which only happens through obedience.

Spiritual understanding occurs when we pass over with Christ by obeying the Father. Then his Word dwells in us, pervades our whole being. It is through this passover that true enlightenment comes.

"Let your face shine on your servant; save me in your unfailing love" (Ps 31:17). We ascend the mount of the Transfiguration *to be saved*, to pass over. We do not ascend to gaze upon some image of our own mind which lulls us into the delights of passive spirituality, or deadens us to the responsibilities of love. We do not seek to "make Christ appear" for our enjoyment. This is magic. We cannot make the true God appear. But when he does it is to draw us into his own divine life. The real experience of Christ on Tabor calls for passing over, not curious contemplation.

Apply the parable of the sower (Mk 4:1-20) to your reading of the Scriptures. Are you "rocky ground"? Are you "thorns"? Or are you "good soil"?

The transfigured Christ manifests himself in the Scriptures to draw us into his glorious life. In some way he is always speaking to us about our death which is to be accomplished in Jerusalem.

Origen

Commentary on Numbers   SF 111-112

"The law turns into an Old Testament only for those who insist on understanding it according to the flesh; and for them it has necessarily become old and feeble because it is separated from its sources of life. But for us, who understand and interpret it spiritually and according to the Gospel, it is always new; indeed both Testaments are new for us, not because of age but because of newness of understanding."

Origen

Commentary on Numbers — SET 111-112

CHAPTER NINE

"And A Voice Came Out Of The Cloud, 'This Is My Beloved Son With Whom I Am Well-Pleased. Listen To Him.'"

Listening To Christ In The Scriptures Is Obeying Him

UP TO NOW we have basically been considering the positive approaches to Scripture: it is a theophany of the glorious Christ; it is an intimate conversation with him as members of the Church; silence and prayer help greatly to hear his Voice. With the theme of Scripture as an exodus into the life of Christ we are led into the consideration of that other "mystery" in the Bible, "the mystery of iniquity," "the secret power of lawlessness" (2 Th 2:7) which is at work in us. Until after the resurrection the apostles did not listen to Christ as the Father told them. This is basically what sin is: not listening to God. On Tabor, this deafness to the voice of the Father was expressed in their drowsiness and their fear. Later it was expressed in their running away from Christ (except for John) when the Lord "was handed over into the hands of men" (cf. Mk 14:50, Jn 19:25-27). Let us consider each of these aspects of the "power of lawlessness."

I do not think that there is a better explanation of what each and every line of the Scriptures is all about than: "This is my beloved Son with whom I am well-pleased. Listen to him." Each line of Scripture is an expression of the Eternal Father's Word, calling us to listen to that Word so that we might "have life in abundance" (Jn 10:10).

It is common knowledge now that, in both Greek and Hebrew, the word "obedience" refers to one harmonious action of *understanding and doing* what one hears. Obedience means to "hear completely," as when our parents said to us: "Didn't you HEAR ME?" "Hear," in this sense (as we all learned quickly!), meant to do immediately what we heard. The centurion in the Gospel also describes the exact meaning: "I say to my servant, 'Go!' and he goes, 'Do this!' and he does it" (Lk 7:8). On the part of the servant there is no *mere* listening, no disjunction between the command and its prompt implementation. Hearing the command and doing it is one and the same action.

God's Word is this effective Word; he does not indulge in mere talking! God speaks, and things happen. "'Let there be light,' and there was light" (Gn 1:3). "My Word will not return to me void, but will accomplish what I desire" (Is 55:11). Tree, stone, planet, lion, Adam, are all words of God which came into being immediately upon his speaking them. All these creatures — except Adam — do exactly what God spoke; they *are* what God spoke. Only Adam, the human person, in all the universe, does not perfectly express what God spoke. We do not perfectly express the word which we are because we have been given the power to say "No, I will not listen!" Imagine (we don't have to imagine it!) the audacity, the arrogance of it all: We can say no to God's Word!

There are literally thousands of statements in the Bible describing how we refuse to listen to God: "What is this you have done?" (Gn 3:13); "I reared children and brought them up, but they have rebelled against me. . . Israel does not know, my people do not understand" (Is 1:2-3); "For twenty-three years the word of the Lord has come to me and I have spoken to you again and again, but you have not listened" (Jr 25:3). "Hear the Word of the Lord," is the constant cry of the prophets. Our constant reaction is not to listen: "Every man's own word becomes his own oracle and so you distort the words of the living God" (Jr 23:36). Even when the Word himself came and "spoke as no man has ever spoken," even then we preferred the darkness to the light, the confusion of our own minds to the clear voice of God.

One of the most beautiful of all the psalms (119) expresses, in countless ways, the heart's longing to know, listen to, and obey God's voice and will: "I seek you with all my heart; do not let me stray from your commands" (vs. 10); "I will not neglect your word" (vs. 16); "Do not snatch the word of truth from my mouth" (vs. 43); "I have promised to obey your words; I have sought your face with all my heart" (vss. 57-58). If we desire the Word to dwell in us as Jesus said we should, if we want the Father and Jesus to make their home in us, then we must *obey* the Word, *do* what God has asked of us.

The classic statement for what we can do is Isaiah 40:3-5. Without God's help we cannot overcome the "power of lawlessness"; but with his help and our efforts we can prepare the way for his indwelling:

In the desert prepare the way for the Lord;
make straight in the wilderness a highway for our God.
Every valley shall be raised up,
every mountain and hill made low;
the rough ground shall become level,
the rugged places a plain.
And the glory of the Lord will be revealed.

The desert, the wilderness, is the human heart turned away from God; it is the uncircumcised ear which refuses to hear God's voice. The valleys, mountains, hills, rough ground, rugged places, are the sinful areas of lawlessness which have not submitted to the reign of God. Without such submission the "glory of God" cannot be revealed, which is his dwelling within us.

The "valleys" are the dark troughs of the spirit we descend into when we refuse to believe in God's immense love for us:

> when we hate ourselves and foster self-destructive thoughts;
> when we do not believe in God's forgiveness of our sins;
> when we destroy our minds and bodies and those of others by an abuse of God's gifts;
> when we hold onto our sadness, pessimism and despair;
> when we do not believe in Christ and his total victory over evil.

The "mountains and hills" are our pride whereby we exalt ourselves:

> when we refuse to forgive, we who have been forgiven so much;
> when we do not believe the Gospel and think we know better than Eternal Wisdom;
> when we judge others, we who hardly know the motivations of our own twisted hearts;
> when we refuse to serve others, considering it beneath our dignity;
> when we think ourselves better than others;
> when we consciously sin, making ourselves a criterion of the law of God.

The "rough ground" is our lack of love for one another:

when we kill, hate, and defraud one another;
when we envy the gifts of others;
when we boast of our gifts and seek our own glory;
when we keep a record of wrongs and keep throwing them
in each others' faces when we are angry;
when we rejoice in the harm befalling others.

The "rugged and crooked places" are our lack of honesty and sincerity in our relationships with God and others:

when we lie in speech and intention;
when we desire to appear to be what we are not;
when we rationalize our sins into virtues;
when we keep silent out of cowardice where the truth is
concerned;
when we fear human respect more than the displeasure of
God.

It would be easy to find in the Scriptures countless other valleys, mountains, hills, and crooked ways which prevent God from coming into our hearts and block out his radiant glory. The Word of God can only dwell in us through obedience. "Listen, O Israel!" is the constant cry of the prophets. "You who have ears to hear, let him hear!" is the insistent message of Jesus. "This is my Beloved Son, listen to him!" is the plea of the Eternal Father in the Scriptures.

Origen

Homily III, On the Circumcision of Abraham FC 96-100

"But let us lay aside those who, like idols, 'have ears and do not hear and eyes and do not see.' But you, 'O people of God, and a people chosen for an acquisition to expound the virtues of the Lord,' take up the circumcision worthy of the word of God in your ears and in your lips and in your heart and in the foreskin of your flesh and in all your members together.

"For let your ears be circumcised according to the word of God that they may not receive the voice of the detractor, that they may not be open to false accusations, to a lie, to an irritation. Let them be shut up and closed 'lest they hear the judgment of blood' or stand open to lewd songs and sounds of the theater. Let them receive nothing obscene, but let them be turned away from every corrupt scene.

"This is the circumcision with which the Church of Christ circumcises the ears of its infants. Those, I believe, are the ears which the Lord was seeking in his hearers when he said, 'He who has ears to hear, let him hear.' For no one with uncircumcised and impure ears can hear the pure words of wisdom and truth.

Homily III, On the Circumcision of Abraham — FC 96, 100

CHAPTER TEN

"Peter And His Companions Were Sleepy, But When They Woke Up They Saw His Glorious Appearance"

Sin As Obscuring The Light Of The Glorious Appearance

SIN IS the refusal to obey God; it has many effects and consequences on the totality of our being. One effect is that sin blocks out the light, the knowledge of God, the ability to see his glorious appearance. I take the sleep of the apostles on Tabor as a symbol of this spiritual blindness.

When our spiritual and bodily senses are turned away from God through disobedience we are in a deep, spiritual sleep, and we are not conscious of the glorious presence of God. This was the sleep of Peter and his companions. The aftermath of the Transfiguration revealed that they were still dominated by fear and cowardice in acknowledging their Lord, and in following him to Calvary. Their "awakening" on Tabor was a pure act of mercy, and not due in any way to their conversion of heart. Anytime he wishes, God can reveal himself to us in this way, whether we are in sin or not. What we seek is the growing and permanent awareness of Christ's presence which results from an obedient life.

For Christians, to "know God" is not a matter of abstract

knowledge or technique; it is a matter of love. True and living knowledge of God flows from obeying his Word:

> We know that we have come to know him if we obey his commands. The man who says, "I know him," but does not do what he commands is a liar, and the truth is not in him. But if anyone obeys his word, God's love is truly made complete in him. This is how we know we are in him: Whoever claims to live in him must walk as Jesus did. (1 Jn 2:3-6)

> Whoever hears my commands and obeys them, he is the one who loves me. He who loves me will be loved by my Father, and I too will love him and show myself to him. (Jn 14:21)

Love and obedience is the way to the "showing," the appearance of Christ, not as a sporadic episode but as a permanent interior dwelling — "we will come and make our home with him" (Jn 14:23).

God lights up our darkness (Ps 18:29). He is our light and salvation (Ps 27:1). His word is a lamp for our feet (Ps 119:105) and a light for our eyes (Ps 19:9). But this light of God illumines our darkness only if we obey his word, pass over from darkness to light through *conversion*. As always, Eternal Wisdom says it exactly: "I am the light of the world. He who *follows me* does not walk in darkness but has the light of life" (Jn 8:12). Jesus becomes our light — appears — if we follow him, do what he says. The "mystery of iniquity" within us makes us flee from the light:

> This is the verdict: Light has come into the world, but men loved the darkness instead of the light because their deeds were evil. Everyone who does evil hates the light, and will not come into the light for fear that his deeds will be exposed. But whoever lives by the truth comes into the

light, so that it may be seen plainly that what he has done
has been done through God. (Jn 3:19-21)

It is not easy to look steadily into the face of Christ in the
Scriptures and allow his words and gaze to illuminate our
lives. Like Adam and Eve in the garden, sin makes us hide
from God: his gaze will expose our disobedience.

Not only does sin make us flee the light; it causes darkness and spiritual blindness to grow:

> . . . those who leave the path of honesty to walk the road of
> darkness. (Pr 2:13)

> No, wisdom will never make its way into a crafty soul, nor
> stay in a body that is in debt to sin. (Ws 1:4)

> Some are living in gloom and darkness . . . for defying the
> orders of God. (Ps 107:10-11)

> They are misled. Their malice makes them blind. (Wis
> 2:21)

Read here the magnificent 28th chapter in Job which ends:

> Where does wisdom come from? Where does understand-
> ing dwell?. . . God alone understands the way to it and he
> alone knows where it dwells. . . The fear of the Lord — that
> is wisdom, and to shun evil is understanding. (Jb 28:20, 23,
> 28)

We should always assume as fact that much of our being
is still spiritually asleep. Look at a crucifix. How can we look
at God hanging on a cross and not be affected? It's due to
our spiritual blindness. There is a universe of darkness still
between us and our God. When we open the Scriptures, it

should be our intention to dispel more of this darkness: we should always *presume* there is still much darkness within us. Otherwise, we will remain in our spiritual slumber.

The parable of the virgins (Mt 25:1-13) is another symbol of this spiritual slumber: they had not been living a life of charity and obedience so as to give them access to the banquet. There is a terrible line at the end of the parable which we should often meditate on to rouse us from our sleep: "I tell you the truth, I don't know you."

If disobedience blocks out from us the light of God, it is also true that our sin makes us unrecognizable to God — "I don't know you." Jesus specifically connects this with our failure to do his will: "Then you will say, 'we ate and drank with you, and you taught in our streets.' But he will reply, ' I don't know you or where you are from. Away from me, all you evil-doers' " (Lk 13:26-27).

In Luke 8:21 Jesus says, "My mother and brothers are those who hear God's word and put it into practice." Only those who do his Father's will, only those for whom this will is their food (Jn 4:34), are truly "known" to God. Those who do not obey his will are unrecognizable to him as his children. To read the Scriptures is to have a desire to be roused from our spiritual blindness and sleep so that we can both know and be known by God.

Origen

Homily VII, On Genesis FC

"But let us beware, for frequently we . . . lie around the well of 'living water,' that is around the divine Scriptures and err in them. We hold the books and we read them, but we do not touch upon the spiritual sense. And, therefore, there is need for tears and incessant prayer that the Lord may open our eyes, because even the eyes of those blind men who were sitting in Jericho would not have been opened unless they had cried out to the Lord. And what am I saying? That our eyes, which are already open, might be opened? For Jesus came to open the eyes of the blind. Our eyes, therefore, are opened and the veil of the letter of the Law is removed. But I fear that we ourselves may close them again in a deeper sleep while we are not watchful in the spiritual meaning, nor are we disturbed so that we dispel sleep from our eyes and contemplate things which are spiritual, that we might not err with the carnal people set around the water itself. But rather let us be watchful and say with the prophet: 'If I shall give sleep to my eyes and slumber to my eyelids, or rest to my temples, until I find a place for the Lord, a tabernacle for the God of Jacob.' To him be glory and sovereignty forever and ever.   Amen."

CHAPTER ELEVEN

"A Bright Cloud Overshadowed Them, And They Were Afraid As They Entered The Cloud"

Awe And Reverence In Approaching The Scriptures

ONE OF THE FIRST CONSEQUENCES of sin is the wrong kind of fear of God: "I heard you in the garden and I was afraid because I was naked, and so I hid" (Gn 3:10). Another effect of sin — or rather, of a lack of awareness of sin — is no reverence at all.

When we approach Christ our God in the Scriptures we should be filled with awe and reverence and respect. In the Gospels, only unbelievers casually saunter up to Jesus, either to dispute with him or reject him; only unbelievers invite him into their homes without showing him the customary marks of respect.

People with faith say, "Lord, I am not worthy for you to come into my home." After the resurrection, upon meeting the glorified Christ, the first thing the disciples do is worship him (Mt 28:17). Whenever we open the Scriptures we should bow down and worship the Lord.

But as Christians, we do not tremble as the Israelites did at Mt. Sinai. Chrysostom points out the difference: "When the Lord threatens, he comes in the darkness of clouds, as on

Sinai. But here (on Tabor), since he wished not to chastise but to teach, a bright cloud appears."

Peter, on Tabor, had not yet passed over into Christ. He was still in the dense cloud of Exodus out of which they were told: "Be careful that you do not go up the mountain or touch the foot of it. Whoever touches the mountain shall surely be put to death" (Ex 19:12). Peter was still in the dark cloud of 1 K 8:10-11 where the power of the Lord's glory was so intense the priests could not fulfill their service. Far from forbidding the apostles to touch Mt. Tabor, Jesus invites them to come up. The Letter to the Hebrews says it magnificently:

> You have not come to a mountain that cannot be touched and that is burning with fire; to darkness, gloom and storm; to a trumpet blast or to such a voice speaking words that those who heard it begged that no further word be spoken to them because they could not bear what was commanded: "Even if an animal touches the mountain, it must be stoned." The sight was so terrifying that Moses said, "I am trembling with fear." But you have come to Mount Zion, to the heavenly Jerusalem, the city of the living God. You have come to thousands upon thousands of angels in joyful assembly, to the church of the firstborn, whose names are written in heaven. You have come to God, the judge of all men, to the spirits of righteous men made perfect, to Jesus the mediator of a new covenant, and to the sprinkled blood that speaks a better word than the blood of Abel. (Heb 12:18-24)

All is contained in the phrase, "You have come to Jesus." Jesus is the bright cloud, the mountain. It is his blood which, unlike Abel's which cried out for vengeance, is eternally presented to the Father graciously pleading for mercy. If we have been made alive in Christ, if Christ our hope of glory dwells in us, then in some real way we are already in the heavenly Jerusalem, "seated with him in the heavenly realms" (Ep 2:6).   Christ is the fulfillment of all the inner sanctuaries and holies of holies that ever existed. The belief of the early Christians was that, in Christ, they had been invited to enter this sanctuary.

They used a special word for this confidence or boldness in entering God's presence. In the culture of their day it referred to a free citizen's right to go before a magistrate and plead his own case. "In Christ and through faith in him we may approach God with freedom and confidence. . ." (Ep 3:12).   "Therefore, brothers, since we have confidence to enter the Most Holy Place by the blood of Jesus . . . let us draw near to God with a sincere heart in full assurance of faith, having our hearts sprinkled to cleanse us from a guilty conscience and having our bodies washed with pure water" (Heb 10:19, 22).

The modern temptation here is flippancy, and an over-familiarity which stems from spiritual obtuseness and immaturity. It is not the confidence of which I have just spoken, but rather a real lack of true reverence.

Jesus is not our "buddy." In the Gospels, whenever people worship him, he accepts it as his right and due. He never says (as Peter and Paul had to say on occasion), "Get up, don't bow down before me. I am a man like yourself" (cf. Ac 3:12, 10:26, 14:15).   Yes, Jesus is our Brother. Yes, he calls us his friends and not servants any longer. But he is always Lord of Lords, and true God of true God. Whenever we approach him it is always on our knees in awe and reverence.

But it is not the awe and terror of Sinai. It is the worship of so many men and women in the Gospels — lepers, officials, public sinners — who were attracted into his presence by his love and mercy but who nonetheless first bowed down and worshipped him. As God, Jesus requires our worship, which is only right and just. But he invites us up the mountain to teach and heal us, not to frighten us.

The word used for the cloud "overshadowing them" in Luke is the same word he uses for the overshadowing of the Virgin Mary, "the power of the Most High will overshadow you" (Lk 1:35). This is not the terrible, dark cloud of Sinai but the bright, merciful cloud of the Father enveloping his children in the divine/human embrace of his Son. We should approach, therefore, with great confidence and trust; we should always, however, take off our shoes, "for the place is holy" (Ex 3:5).

Origen

Commentary on John   SF 112

"Whoever drinks from Jacob's well will thirst again, but whoever drinks from the water which Jesus gives has within him a fountain of water springing into eternal life. With this in mind let us examine further how much of a distinction can be made between the benefit obtained by those who have a direct and intimate relationship with the truth itself and the benefit we think comes to us from the scriptures, if they are exactly understood.

"For the more noble and divine mysteries of God are in part not contained in scripture and in part not attainable by human voice and human language. . . Consider then, if it is not possible that the well of Jacob is the whole of scripture, but that the water from Jesus is that which is above what is written. But it is not possible for all to search out the things which are above what is written, but only for the one who has become assimilated to them."

CHAPTER TWELVE

"Master, It Is Good For Us To Be Here. Let Us Put Up Three Tents. . ."

Scripture As Call To Painful Mission

ORIGEN SAYS that Peter's remark was certainly not from the Holy Spirit since Scripture itself says he didn't know what he was saying!

The Fathers generally see Peter's remark as a fear of the cross, a fear of what was going to happen to Jesus in Jerusalem. Origen again:

> Because Peter had heard that the Lord must go to Jerusalem, he was still fearful for Christ. But since his reproof, he does not again dare to say, "Lord, be merciful to yourself"; but indirectly he conveys the same state of mind by other means. For when he sees this place of solitude and quiet, he thinks that . . . here would be a suitable place to remain. He desires even to remain there always, and so he speaks of dwelling places, saying, "Let us build, etc." For he thought that if they did this, the Lord would not go to Jerusalem; and if he did not go to Jerusalem, he would not die. There, in Jerusalem, he knew the scribes lay in wait for him. They would be well hidden here, so that none of the persecutors would know where they were.

> It was to turn him aside from the dispensation whose chief
> characteristic was suffering . . . to draw Jesus away . . . to
> abide on the Mount with Moses and Elias.

We have spoken of Christ in the Scriptures calling us to
pass over into his divine life, calling us to obey his Father.
Both calls (which are really one) often entail suffering. Fear
of suffering, therefore, is one of the obstacles to having the
Word dwell within us. It is not entirely due to sin. Even the
Sinless One dreaded his ordeal: "Father, if it be possible, let
this cup pass. But not as I will but as you will" (Lk
22:42).   But much of this fear comes from sin and our
disorientation from God.

There is a whole world to be restored to God — people to
be liberated from Egypt, false idols to be torn down, God's
words of fire to be proclaimed to his people, forgiveness and
healing to be mediated to all. So when God manifests himself it is not simply for our consolation and wonderment. It
often entails a painful mission.

In the earliest appearances of God to Abraham he is
asked to leave his country (Gn 12:1) and to sacrifice his only
son (Gn 22:1-19).   Moses is told to go to Egypt and bring
the Israelites out of bondage (Ex 3:4-4:17).   Samuel's first
assignment is to speak a harsh word to Eli, his spiritual
father (Is 3:1-18).   And all the prophets had their harsh
words to deliver. John the Baptist must preach repentance,
and Jesus must go to Jerusalem. The Lord says to Ananias
that Paul is a chosen instrument, but that "I will show him
how much he must suffer for my name" (Ac 9:16).   After
Isaiah's awesome vision of the holiness of God the voice of
the Lord says, "Whom shall I send? And who will go for us?"
(Is 6:8).

When people receive a theophany in the Scriptures,
often a painful mission is connected with it: the vision is not

merely for their contemplation and delight. In his weakness, this is the mistake Peter made: to want to hold onto the consolation, and forget about the going to Jerusalem. "Lord, it is wonderful to be here!" Yes, it is wonderful to be with Jesus, and Jesus delights to be with us. But in this world there is too much to be done, too much pain to be relieved, too many people who have not heard the Good News. We shall delight with Jesus forever on the eternal mountains. Now is the time for all of us — you, me — to go to Jerusalem.

So, do we go to the Scriptures to be consoled, or to learn the will of God? This will of God often entails suffering and pain. The intimate followers of Jesus are supposed to know this. It is the crowds, the uninformed, the superficial, who think otherwise.

The day after the Transfiguration, when the crowds were ooohing and aaahing over Jesus — "marveling" — the Lord turned and said to his disciples what he had been trying to communicate to them all week: "Listen! Don't be misled by all this naivete and euphoria. I'm going to be betrayed into the hands of men. You are my close followers. You above all must understand the real situation: it is through my suffering and death that I will accomplish my Father's plan" (cf. Lk 9:43-44).

This call to the cross is first and foremost the interior conversion of the heart, the interior passing over and obedience. But life is not only interior. The call of God will entail some painful mission for each of us — the far country of Abraham, the Egypt of Moses will take a different form, but it will be actual and demanding. Jesus knows we need Tabor experiences once in a while, but we are not meant to remain there. Isaiah's response is the only one worthy of a creature before its God: "Here I am. Send me" (Is 6:8).   "Here I am, glorious Christ! Let the light of your face illumine my whole being. Yes, I am afraid of Jerusalem. But stay with me when

I descend the mountain and I will follow you wherever you lead. I want to be a true disciple of yours. I know I cannot be a disciple unless I give up all I possess — the delights of Tabor, especially. Only stay with me. Stay with me."

Origen

Commentary on Leviticus   SF 103, 105

"We have often pointed out that there is a threefold mode of under-standing in the holy scripture: a historical, a moral, and a mystical. We understand from this that there is in scripture a body, a soul and a spirit.

"Therefore just as 'the seen and the unseen' (2 Cor 4:18), earth and heaven, soul and flesh, body and spirit are related to each other, and this world is made up of these relationships, so too must it be believed that holy scripture is made up of seen and unseen things. It consists of a body, namely, the visible letter, and of a soul which is the meaning found within it, and of a spirit by which it also has something of the heavenly in it, as the Apostle says: 'They serve as a copy and shadow of the heavenly sanctuary' (Heb 8:5). Since this is so, calling upon God who made the soul and the body and the spirit of scripture — the body for those who came before us, the soul for us, and the spirit for those who 'in the age to come will receive the inheritance of eternal life' (Lk 18:30) by which they will come to the heavenly things and the truth of the law — let us seek out not the letter but the soul. . . If we do this we will also ascend to the spirit."

CHAPTER THIRTEEN

"When The Disciples Heard This They Fell On Their Faces"

Approaching Christ In The Scriptures As Sinners

As PARADOXICAL AS IT MAY SEEM, *the radical* remedy for our blindness which obscures the light of God, for our avoidance of the cross, for our servile fear of God, and for our refusal to obey, is the acceptance, admission, and realization of the truth *that we are sinners.* The human person is more or less conscious not only of some primordial sin and guilt but of personal sin and guilt as well. Behind all the psychological jargon, this is ultimately why we hide from God in the garden. Therefore, the most truthful and authentic stance of the person in face of the divine is an awareness of sin and unworthiness.

Isaiah's reaction to his vision of the All-Holy was, "Woe to me! I am ruined! I am a man of unclean lips," that is, sinful. But the seraph touches the prophet's mouth with a live coal and says, "See, this has touched your lips! Your guilt is taken away and your sin is atoned for" (Is 6:5-7).

When Simon Peter experienced the presence of the Divine in the miraculous catch of fish "he fell at Jesus' knees and said, 'Go away from me, Lord; I am a sinful man' " (Lk 5:8).

When Jesus told the story of the Pharisee and the Publican praying in the temple he said it was the following prayer which put a person in the right relationship with God: "O Lord, be merciful to me a sinner" (Lk 18:13). The whole tradition in Eastern Christianity of the Jesus Prayer ("Lord Jesus Christ, Son of the living God, have mercy on me, a sinner") is based on this teaching of the Lord.

Jesus frequently forgives the sins of people who come to him, often without their even asking (Lk 7:48; Mt 9:2). He knows that such forgiveness is our deepest need, however else we may understand our reason for approaching him.

The Psalms are filled with petitions for the forgiveness of sins (cf. Ps 51); and seeking reconciliation for sin is one of the constant themes of the prophets: "Though your sins are like scarlet, they shall be as white as snow" (Is 1:18).

When we come before God we must be truthful. And the truth is that we are sinners: "For I know my transgressions, and my sin is always before me" (Ps 51:5). Sin is the cause of resistance to hearing the glorious Christ speak to us. Sin is the root cause of our spiritual blindness, of our servile fear of God and of the cross. Why do we "love darkness" (Jn 3:19) instead of the light streaming from the face of Christ Jesus? Because we are sinners. The acceptance of our state of being sinners is the *radical cure* for each of these obstacles.

The Pharisees were spiritually blind to the light of God because they believed they were perfect and without sin. The truth is that, not only are we sinners but, there is still much darkness and sin in us of which we are unaware: "Who can discern his errors? Forgive my hidden faults" (Ps 19:13). It is this realization and acceptance that we are still burdened with many impurities and unrecognized failings which allows the light of God to penetrate. If we know we are still in darkness, then there is hope for us. If we say, "we see," then we are in serious spiritual blindness (cf. Jn 9:41).

Acceptance of our sinfulness actually heals our fear of God. It was the sinners who ran to Jesus because they knew he came for sinners, that he loved sinners, and so they came to have their sins forgiven. I believe it's our refusal to accept our sinfulness which makes us fear God. The often terrible and crippling fear of God, which binds so many people, results from approaching a *terrible God*. The modern approach is to deny sin, and then everything is fine. The Gospel approach is to admit our sins and come to the *merciful Christ*. We cannot experience God's merciful love unless we admit our sins. Then our sins no longer make us hide from God; we are drawn to him by his mercy.

Acceptance of the fact that I'm a sinner is the great key to the acceptance and even understanding of suffering. If I am a sinner, then the sufferings that come my way are just: I can accept them as penance for my sins. And the evil in the world? Most of it is due to disobedience to God, and hence to sin. Through it God seeks to turn people back to him. In Psalm 51:12-14, the "pure heart," the "steadfast spirit," the "restoration of joy," the "willing spirit," the "staying of the Holy Spirit" — are all the fruits bestowed on the contrite heart aware of forgiveness.

The essence of sin is not obeying the Word of God. Admitting that we disobey God is what opens the floodgates of grace and enables us to respond to God's Word. "God gives grace to the humble but resists the proud." If we don't admit that we are proud we don't ask for help, and so cannot receive it.

It is the admission of sin that brings us to our knees. When we reach the stage of weeping for our sins, the stage of helplessness to save ourselves, then God will come with his grace. Until this spiritual weeping occurs we are blind, and are living mostly on human will-power. Read Psalm 32 here. It is unacknowledged sin which is the cause of much of our "wasting away . . . and groaning all the day long" (vs. 3). "But then I acknowledged my sin to you . . . and you forgave the guilt of my sin" (vs. 5).

Read the 42nd chapter of Job. It was only after Job repented in dust and ashes that he saw he was holding forth on matters he could not understand. Before he repented he said he only knew God "by hearsay." After repentance he sees God with his own eyes. Tears of true repentance wash our eyes of illusions about our relationship with God. Repentance allows us to see that relationship in truth.

The great masters of the spiritual life called awareness and acceptance of one's sinfulness "true knowledge." St. Anthony of the Desert said that true knowledge is knowing the difference between good and evil.

In an age when sin is being denied, and we are struggling to offset a fear approach to God, we dare not forget that Jesus has come to save us from our *sins*. The resolution of this fear is not to deny sin but to believe in a most merciful Christ. There is a profound and life-giving way to approach Jesus as sinners which leads to joy and real freedom. This approach is the principal way the Word (who is the Savior) comes to dwell in us.

Origen

Commentary on the Song of Songs
SF 109

"Each and every letter of the gospel gives life to the scribes (if I may call them that) of the gospels. But the spirit which soars above the nature of the letters enlightens even more, with an action that is more divine, those from whom the gospel is not veiled. . . For a certain benefit comes to those who believe in the scriptures; but they who see how the 'curtain' of the scripture is torn 'from top to bottom' (Mt 27:51), and who see what is within, are filled with a greater knowledge."

CHAPTER FOURTEEN

"But Jesus Came And Touched Them. 'Get Up,' He Said. 'Don't Be Afraid' "

The Touch Of Jesus Is Necessary To Hear The Scriptures

ST. JEROME SUMS up very nicely both the beginning and end of this little book of mine:

> Since they were lying prone on the earth, unable to rise, he spoke gently to them, and at his touch fear left them, and their trembling limbs became strong again. Those he had healed by the touch of his hand he healed also by his command. He first casts out fear so that he may then give them his teaching.

I said at the very beginning that the goal of approaching the Scriptures is to have our hearts burn within us as Jesus explains himself as the Word along the road of life. We can't hear the Word because of our sins, our estrangement and disorientation from God, our fears and despairs and sorrows. How does the healing begin? It begins by the touch of Jesus.

The touch of Jesus is the Holy Spirit. He is the "finger of God" through which Jesus drove out demons and ushered in the kingdom of God (Lk 11:20). We are all prostrate on the ground until raised by the finger of God. The apostles, who heard Jesus speak during his lifetime, did not understand him until the coming of the Holy Spirit. And when Jesus promises the coming of this Spirit for our enlightenment, mark well what he will do *first*: "When he comes he will convict the world of guilt in regard to sin and righteousness and judgment" (Jn 16:8). Then the Lord speaks those wonderful words about how the word of the prophets will be made more certain, how the light will shine in the dark places of our hearts, and will make the new, everlasting day dawn in us until the morning star rises in our hearts (cf. 2 P 1:19):

> I have much more to say to you, more than you can now bear. But when he, the Spirit of truth, comes, he will guide you into all truth. He will not speak on his own; but he will speak only what he hears, and he will tell you what is yet to come. He will bring glory to me by taking from what is mine and making it known to you. All that belongs to the Father is mine. That is why I said the Spirit will take from what is mine and make it known to you. (Jn 16:12-15)

The Holy Spirit dwells in us through baptism. But just as it's possible to live with a person without knowing him or her very well personally, just as the disciples could live with and hear Jesus speaking but not understand him, so we too can have the Holy Spirit in us without experiencing that deep, personal awareness of Jesus the Spirit desires to effect in us. What Jesus said of the disciples — and were they not baptized since they were baptizing others? (Jn 4:2) — could be said of many baptized Christians: "In a little while you will see me no more, and then after a little while you will see me" (Jn 16:16). There often is a period between our baptism and our actual "seeing" of Jesus, a period before our being touched by the finger of God.

How often people say, "The Scriptures just don't speak to me." Every Christian should be absolutely convinced that "if the Scriptures don't speak to them" there is a fundamental teaching by the Holy Spirit not taking place in them. I hesitate to say more than that. Our life with God is too mysterious. There could be other factors besides sin which prevent this conversation with Jesus through the Scriptures. But surely we can say that it's the Lord's great desire that all his words be explained to us by his Spirit.

How is this instruction by the Spirit obtained? Through prayer: "How much more will your Father in heaven give the Holy Spirit to those who ask him" (Lk 11:13). It is by asking the Holy Spirit to deepen in you all the attitudes I have been describing here. These attitudes open our hearts to the epiphany of God so that the Word can come and dwell in us.

Perhaps at the very center of all these attitudes and movements of the heart is the desire to "see only Jesus," that is, to have Jesus as the absolute center of our whole life and existence. He has told us that we cannot be his disciples unless we leave everything for his sake. Jesus is our Lord and God. Our longing to have him *really be such*, to have every aspect of our lives subject to his Spirit and reign, *this is the act* which opens the depth of our spirits to the touch of God.

An experience of the Holy Spirit (which people sometimes today call the "baptism in the Holy Spirit") can be a *beginning* of this conversation with Jesus in the Scriptures; but for the deepening and ongoing conversation we must struggle all our lives against the sin and darkness within us. 1 Peter speaks about our birth "not of perishable seed, but of imperishable, through the living and enduring word of God. . . This is the word that was preached to you"

(1 P 1:23, 25). But the author goes on to say that once we have "tasted that the Lord is good" (1 P 2:3), we must "rid (ourselves) of all malice and all deceit, hypocrisy, envy, and slander of every kind. Like newborn babies, crave pure spiritual milk, so that by it you may grow up in your salvation" (1 P 2:1-2).   The pure spiritual milk is the instruction in Jesus' words by the Holy Spirit.

   It is on this note of "growing up in salvation" that I would like to close. The indwelling of the Word in every part of our being will entail a life-long struggle. This total indwelling is God's will and plan for us, and therefore he will help us. God's will *can* become our food as it was for Jesus: "My food is to do the will of him who sent me" (Jn 4:34).   Then one day, when we meet Jesus, we will hear, not the terrible words of unrecognition — "I don't know you" (Mt 25:12) — but the words of recognition, "Come, you blessed of my Father!" (Mt 25:34).   May this little book help to bring you to that blessed meeting!

Origen

Commentary on Matthew ANF

"They were sore afraid at the supernatural sight . . . at He who said,
'A man shall not see my face and live.' Not having been able to
endure the radiance of the Word, they humbled themselves. . .; but
after the touch of the Word, lifting up their eyes, they saw Jesus only
and no other."

APPENDICES

APPENDICES

Appendix A

The Three Synoptic Accounts Of The Transfiguration

MATTHEW 17:1-8

1 And after six days
Jesus took with him
Peter and James and
John his brother, and
led them up a high
mountain apart.

2 And he was transfig-
ured before them,
and his face shone
like the sun,
and his garments be-
came white as light.

3 And behold, there
appeared to them
Moses and Elijah, talk-
ing with him.

MARK 9:2-8

2 And after six days
Jesus took with him
Peter and James and
John, and
led them up a high
mountain apart
by themselves,
and he was transfig-
ured before them,

and his garments be-
came glistening, in-
tensely white, as no
fuller on earth could
bleach them.

4 And there appeared
to them Elijah with
Moses; and they were
talking with Jesus.

LUKE 9:28-36

28 Now about eight days
after these sayings he
took with him Peter and
John and James and
went upon the
mountain to pray.
And as he was praying,
the appearance of his
countenance was altered,

and his raiment be-
came dazzling white.

30 And behold, two men
talked with him, Moses
and Elijah, who appeared
in glory and spoke of his
departure, which he was to
accomplish in Jerusalem.
Now Peter and those who
were with him were heavy
with sleep but kept awake,
and they saw his glory and
the two men who stood
with him. And as the men
were parting from him,

4 And Peter said to
 Jesus, "Lord, it is well
that we are here; if you
wish I will make three
booths here, one for you
and one for Moses and
one for Elijah."

5 He was still speaking,
 when lo, a bright
cloud overshadowed
them

and a voice from the
cloud said, "This is my
beloved Son, with whom
I am well pleased; listen
to him." When the
disciples heard this,
they fell on their faces
and were filled with awe.
But Jesus came and
touched them, saying,
"Rise, and have no fear."
And when they lifted up
their eyes, they saw no
one but only Jesus.

5 And Peter said to
 Jesus, "Master, it is
well that we are here;
let us make three booths,
one for you and one for
Moses and one for
Elijah." For he did not
know what to say, for
they were exceedingly
afraid.

7 And a cloud over-
 shadowed them,

and a voice came out of
the cloud, "This is my
beloved Son; listen to
him."

8 And suddenly looking
 around they no longer
saw any one with them
but Jesus only.

Peter said to Jesus,
"Master, it is well that we
are here; let us make three
booths, one for you and
one for Moses and one for
Elijah" — not knowing
what he said.

34 And as he said this, a
 cloud came and over-
shadowed them; and they
were afraid as they en-
tered the cloud. And a
voice came out of the
cloud, saying, "This is my
Son, my Chosen; listen to
him."

36 And when the voice
 had spoken, Jesus was
found alone. And they
kept silence and told no
one in those days anything
of what they had seen.

Appendix B

Key To Quoted Works Of Origen

ACW   Lawson, R.P. (Trans). *Ancient Christian Writers.* Vol. 26. Origen, the Song of Songs. Commentary and Homilies. Westminster, Maryland: The Newman Press, 1957.

FC   Heine, Ronald E. (Trans). *The Fathers of the Church.* Vol. 71. Origen, Homilies On Genesis and Exodus. Washington, D.C.: The Catholic University of America Press, 1982.

NF   Roberts, Alexander and James Donaldson (Eds). *The Ante-Nicene Fathers.* Vol. IX. Grand Rapids, MI: Wm.B. Eerdmans Publishing Co., 1974.

SF   Von Balthasar, Hans Urs (Trans). *Origen, Spirit and Fire.* A Thematic Anthology of His Writings. Translated from the German by Robert J. Daly, S.J., Washington, D.C.: The Catholic University of America Press, 1984.

Appendix B

Key To Quoted Sources Of Origin

Appendix C

Excerpts From *Dei Verbum*, The Dogmatic Constitution On Divine Revelation

Dei Verbum, the Dogmatic Constitution on Divine Revelation, was promulgated by the Second Vatican Council on November 18, 1965. It is recommended that this entire document be read in conjunction with this book. The following are some excerpts from *Dei Verbum* that have particular relevance to the various chapters of the present work.

——————— *INTRODUCTION* ———————

"The Tradition that comes from the apostles makes progress in the Church, with the help of the Holy Spirit. There is a growth in insight into the realities and words that are being passed on. This comes about in various ways. It comes through the contemplation and study of believers who ponder these things in their hearts. It comes from the intimate sense of spiritual realities which they experience. And it comes from the preaching of those who have received, along with their right of succession in the episcopate, the sure charism of truth. Thus, as the centuries go by, the Church is always advancing towards the plenitude of divine truth, until eventually the words of God are fulfilled in her. The sayings of the Holy Fathers are a witness to the life-giving presence of this

Tradition, showing how its riches are poured out in the practice and life of the Church, her belief and her prayer." DV 8

"The spouse of the incarnate Word, which is the Church, is taught by the Holy Spirit. She strives to reach day by day a more profound understanding of the sacred Scriptures, in order to provide her children with food from the divine words. For this reason also she duly fosters the study of the Fathers, both Eastern and Western, and of the sacred liturgies." DV 23

"Sacred Scripture is the speech of God as it is put down in writing under the breath of the Holy Spirit." DV 9

────── CHAPTER ONE ──────

"The Church always venerated the divine Scriptures as she venerated the Body of the Lord, in so far as she never ceases, particularly in the sacred liturgy, to partake of the bread of life and to offer it to the faithful from the one table of the Word of God and the Body of Christ." DV 21

"In the sacred Scriptures the Father who is in heaven comes lovingly to meet his children and talks to them." DV 21

────── CHAPTER TWO ──────

"Before faith can be exercised, man must have the grace of God to move and assist him; he must have the interior helps of the Holy Spirit, who moves the heart and converts it to God, who opens the eyes of the mind and 'makes it easy for all to accept and believe the truth' (Council of Orange). The same Holy Spirit constantly perfects faith by his gifts, so that revelation may be more and more profoundly understood." DV 5

"It is common knowledge that among all the inspired writings . . . the Gospels have a special place . . . because they are our principal source for the life and teaching of the Incarnate Word, our Savior." DV 18

_____ *CHAPTER THREE* _____

"The task of giving an authentic interpretation of the Word of God, whether in its written form or in the form of Tradition, has been entrusted to the living teaching office of the Church alone. Its authority in this matter is exercised in the name of Jesus Christ. Yet this Magisterium is not superior to the Word of God, but is its servant." DV 10

_____ *CHAPTER FOUR* _____

"Thus God, who spoke in the past, continues to converse with the Spouse of his beloved Son. And the Holy Spirit, through whom the living voice of the Gospel rings out in the Church — and through her in the world — leads believers to the full truth, and makes the Word of Christ dwell in them in all its richness (Col 3:16)." DV 8

_____ *CHAPTER FIVE* _____

"Let them remember, however, that prayer should accompany the reading of sacred Scripture, so that a dialogue takes place between God and man. For, 'we speak to him when we pray; we listen to him when we read the divine oracles' (St. Ambrose)." DV 25

_____ *CHAPTER SIX* _____

"The most intimate truth which this revelation gives us about God and the salvation of man shines forth in Christ, who is himself both the mediator and the sum total of revelation." DV 2

———————— *CHAPTER SEVEN* ————————

"God, the inspirer and author of the books of both testaments, in his wisdom has so brought it about that the New should be hidden in the Old and that the Old should be made manifest in the New. The books of the Old Testament attain and show forth their full meaning in the New Testament, and in their turn shed light on it and explain it."   DV 16

———————— *CHAPTER EIGHT* ————————

"By this revelation the invisible God from the fullness of his love addresses men as his friends and moves among them in order to invite and receive them into his own company."   DV 2

"He revealed that God was with us to deliver us from the darkness of sin and death and to raise us up to eternal life."   DV 4

———————— *CHAPTER NINE* ————————

"The obedience of faith must be given to God as he reveals himself. By faith man freely commits his entire self to God, making the full submission of his intellect and will to God who reveals, and willingly assenting to the Revelation given by him."   DV 5

———————— *CHAPTER TEN* ————————

"Therefore, all clerics, particularly priests of Christ and others who, as deacons or catechists, are officially engaged in the ministry of the Word, should immerse themselves in the Scriptures by constant sacred reading and diligent study. For it must not happen that anyone becomes 'an empty preacher of the Word of God to others, not being a hearer of the Word in his own heart' (St. Augustine)."   DV 25

——— *CHAPTER ELEVEN* ———

"This sacred synod forcefully and specifically exhorts all the Christian faithful . . . to learn 'the surpassing knowledge of Jesus Christ' (Ph 3:8) by frequent reading of the divine Scriptures. 'Ignorance of the Scriptures is ignorance of Christ' (St. Jerome). Let them go gladly, therefore, to the sacred text itself, whether in the sacred liturgy, which is full of the divine words, or in devout reading, or in such suitable exercises and various other helps which, with the approval and guidance of the pastors of the Church, are happily spreading everywhere in our day." DV 25

——— *CHAPTER TWELVE* ———

"God wishes to give eternal life to all those who seek salvation by patience in well-doing (Rm 2:6). In his own time he called Abraham. . . After the era of the patriarchs he taught this nation through Moses and the prophets. . . He taught them to look for the promised Savior. And so throughout the ages he prepared the way for the Gospel. (Then) he sent his Son, the eternal Word who enlightens all men, to dwell among men and to tell them about the inner life of God. Hence, Jesus Christ, sent as 'a man among men,' speaks the words of God (Jn 3:34), and accomplishes the saving work which the Father gave him to do." DV 3-4

——— *CHAPTER THIRTEEN* ———

"Such is the force and power of the Word of God that it can serve the Church as her support and vigor, and the children of the Church as strength for their faith, food for the soul, a pure and lasting fount of spiritual life. Scripture verifies in the most perfect way the words, 'The Word of God is living and active' (Heb 4:12), and 'is able to build you up and to give you the inheritance among all those who are sanctified' (Ac 20:32; 1 Th 2:13)." DV 21

———— *CHAPTER   FOURTEEN* ————

"Hence, in sacred Scripture, without prejudice to God's truth and holiness, the marvelous condescension of eternal wisdom is plain to be seen 'that we may come to know the ineffable loving-kindness of God and see for ourselves how far he has gone in adapting his language with thoughtful concern for our nature' (St. John Chrysostom). Indeed, the words of God, expressed in the words of men, are in every way like human language, just as the Word of the eternal Father, when he took on himself the flesh of human weakness, became like men."   DV 13